Come to Your Senses!

Listening to evocative music, savoring a juicy peach, watching autumn leaves dance against a blue sky, feeling the comforting touch of a loved one—your senses are a source of pure enjoyment. The senses are also the pathways through which you understand and interact with your world. When they are not exercised and appreciated, you lose the vividness which they can bring to the simplest experiences. Life becomes dull when you treat your senses as merely utilitarian—and you miss out on some of the best things that being a human being has to offer.

This book shows you how to reawaken senses you may have been taking for granted to heighten every moment of your life. Fun-to-do exercises will put you in touch with the world of sensuous pleasure that surrounds you every moment. Relish the touch of sun-dried sheets on your skin. Tantalize your palate with unusual foods and taste your favorites with a new awareness. Attune to tiny auditory pleasures that surround you, from the click of computer keys to raindrops hitting a window. Appreciate light, shadow and color with an artist's eye. And stop worrying so much about acting "normal" and being "productive" every minute of your life!

An adventure of the senses awaits you. Take the time to revel in the delight they can bring—and experience the zest and joie de vivre that come from truly living in every moment.

About the Author

Nancy Conger writes: "When I was ten, new lip balms came into the market with vibrant scents that smelled exactly like the fruits each balm represented. I had a friend hold each flavor under my nose while I closed my eyes. To my surprise, though each scent was familiar, I couldn't name it. When I saw the color of the packages, however, I could identify them. It was then I first became fascinated with the interplay of our senses and how we rely on, or ignore, them. Since that time I have collected and created exercises that increase awareness of the senses, and learned techniques that help improve the faculties."

Nancy graduated with English and Music majors from the College of St. Catherine in St. Paul, Minnesota. She has worked several years as a corporate writer, and currently is a manager of employee relations. She plays violin and dabbles in dance, song-writing, visual arts, and new musical instruments.

To Write to the Author

If you wish to contact the author or would like more information about this book, please write to the author in care of Llewellyn Worldwide, and we will forward your request. Both the author and publisher appreciate hearing from you and learning of your enjoyment of this book and how it has helped you. Llewellyn Worldwide cannot guarantee that every letter written to the author can be answered, but all will be forwarded. Please write to:

Nancy Conger
% Llewellyn Worldwide
P.O. Box 64383-K160, St. Paul, MN 55164-0383, U.S.A.
Please enclose a self-addressed, stamped envelope for reply, or $1.00 to cover costs. If outside the U.S.A., enclose international postal reply coupon.

Free Catalog from Llewellyn

For more than 90 years Llewellyn has brought its readers knowledge in the fields of metaphysics and human potential. Learn about the newest books in spiritual guidance, natural healing, astrology, occult philosophy and more. Enjoy book reviews, new age articles, a calendar of events, plus current advertised products and services. To get your free copy of *Llewellyn's New Worlds of Mind and Spirit*, send your name and address to:

Llewellyn's New Worlds of Mind and Spirit
P.O. Box 64383-K160, St. Paul, MN 55164-0383, U.S.A.

Llewellyn's Whole Life Series

Sensuous Living

Expand Your Sensory Awareness

Nancy Conger

1995
Llewellyn Publications
St. Paul, Minnesota 55164-0383, U.S.A.

FIRST EDITION
First Printing, 1995

Cover design: Anne Marie Garrison
Cover photograph: Lynne Menturweck
Interior illustrations: Nyease Somersett
Book design, layout, and editing: Pamela Henkel

Library of Congress Cataloging-in-Publication Data
Conger, Nancy, 1962—
    Sensuous living : expand your sensory awareness / Nancy
    Conger.— 1st ed.
          p.   c.m.— (Llewellyn's whole life series)
    Includes bibliographical references.
    ISBN 1-56718-160-0
    1. Senses and sensation. 2. Sensory stimulation. 3. Sensuality.
    I. Title. II. Series.
BF233.C586 1995
152.1—dc20   95-12263
                                                        CIP

Llewellyn Publications
A Division of Llewellyn Worldwide, Ltd.
P.O. Box 64383, St. Paul, MN 55164-0383

About Llewellyn's Whole Life Series

Each of us is born into a body. But an amazing number of us lack anything beyond the most utilitarian connection with our physical beings. Yet, being "in touch" with the body—being aware of the senses' connection to our thoughts, emotions, dreams and spirits—is integral to holistic living.

Instead of taking the intellect or the spirit as a starting point, books of the Whole Life Series focus on the physical—sensation and bodily health—and how it is inextricably linked with the health of our minds and souls.

What does the physical have to do with the emotional or the spiritual? Everything. We are as much beings of the Earth as we are beings of the stars ... our senses and connection to our bodies are just as integral to our physical, emotional and spiritual well-being as is our connection to our higher selves.

The old doctrines, which regard the physical as inferior to the spiritual, may have made sense for the medieval ascetic—but, much like the medieval belief that the Sun orbited the Earth, those beliefs have been supplanted by more enlightened ones. Fortunately. Because it is impossible to truly feel that we *belong* in the universe, just as much as the ground we walk on and the air we breathe, until we entirely accept our own natures as physical and spiritual creatures. This book will help you heal the split between will and understanding and further your journey to wholeness, the place where body, mind and spirit are integrated and healed. Access your internal source of wisdom, love and healing through the techniques presented here for heightened mind and body awareness ... and become so much more than the sum of your parts.

Table of Contents

Introduction 1
How to Use This Book; Why a Book on Sensuous Living?;
Benefits of a Sensuous Life; What is a Sensual Person?;
Keys to Sensual Enjoyment

1: Smell: The Primeval Sense 15
Why Is It so "Primitive?"; Smell and Food; Haven't I
Smelled You Here Before?; Happy Smell, Sad Smell;
Medicinal Smell; Improve Your Sniffer; Let's Practice!

2: Touch: The Essential Sense 39
What is Skin?; Touch and Grow; Touching the Emotions;
The Sex Connection; A Touch of Health; What a Pain;
"Touchy" Communication; Unlearning the Silly Rules;
Let's Touch!

3: Taste: The Cultural Sense 75
In the Tongue Groove; Good to Eat, or Good to Think?
Food Taboos; Kiss Me or Pass the Oysters; Food Talk;
Barriers to Good Taste; Tasting the Good Life

4: Hearing: The Social Sense 105
The Amazing Ear; Do You Hear What I Hear?
The Nature of Sound; Is That Music?; Ear Enemy No. 1:
Noise; What's That Again? Preserving Your Hearing;
Hear Hear!

5: Vision: The Dominant Sense 133
What's in an Eye?; Vital Light; Two Eyes, One Scene; Now
You See It, Now You Don't ; Clues to Perception; What
Affects Vision?; How to Develop Eagle Eyes;
Fun with Vision

6: The Unacknowledged Senses 163
Balance; Balancing Fun; Solar Sense; Getting Your
Fill; Magnetic Sense; ESP; Trigeminal Sense; Synesthesia;
Electrical Sense; Proprioreceptive (Kinesthetic) Sense

7: Symphony of the Senses 185
Seeking Sensual Experience; Integrating the Senses;
The Sensual Reminder

Bibliography 197

Introduction

This book was created to encourage people to claim a way of life that has been lost to many in today's society. It is a guide for using and improving the senses to enjoy life more fully. While most of us are unabashedly sensual as children, societal norms gradually train us to forget our natural state. My childhood overflowed with sensual experiences: swimming in rivers, molding clay, digging holes, playing instruments. I have an art teacher for a mother and outdoorsman for a father, so I learned at an early age to experience beauty all around me in nature. I didn't just look at trees; I fingered roots while transplanting and gathered spiny cones for artwork, rustling through leaves for particular beauties. I didn't just eat fish; I felt their protective slime and rough scales,

saw their red insides, smelled their lake odor, and listened to them sizzle in oil. I learned to enjoy simple things, such as the smell of juice and tea, a cold glass against my face, or a hot mug between my hands.

It did not take long, however, to see that the rest of the world viewed open sensory enjoyment differently. Smelling one's food was rude. Touching someone's silk sleeve encroached on personal space. Listening to cookie dough bake was just plain weird. To accommodate societal expectations that subvert our natural desire to sense, we each develop an "action editor" that diverts sensual impulse so that we fit in. I offer this book as a pink slip for your action editor—a permission slip for you to reclaim the senses and enjoyment they bring.

— How to Use this Book —

Get ready to play! Through understanding and using your senses, you will rediscover their power. You will learn simply by reading, but the full experience requires your participation in the activities. Although you may end up using some of the activities only once for awareness, others you may want to incorporate into your daily way of life. When you come upon an exercise that urges you to do something promptly, do it on the spot. For others that require set-up or materials you do not have on hand, do them when you can. The first reading of this book will give you an understanding and introduction to senses and sensuality; the second time through will allow you to just have fun with the games and exercises. Some of the activities are interesting to do at a party or work.

Use the activities and tips in this book to create your own journey into sensual living.

— Why a Book on Sensuous Living? —

Our main senses—taste, touch, sight, hearing, and smell—are the pathways by which we understand and interact with our world. Essential to relationships, they allow us to see facial expressions, touch one another, smell each other's faint, warm scents, and hear words and tones of voice. They protect us, warning of a hot stove, rotten food, or bitter poison. They enable pure enjoyment: hearing a joke, listening to music, savoring food, massaging our skin, watching a play. Like our muscles and minds, our senses work their best when we use them regularly. When they are not exercised and appreciated, we lose the bright edge they give life. Life becomes dull, and our senses become nothing more than utilitarian functions to which we pay little attention. Surprisingly, in an age where stimuli bombard us more than ever, we use our senses less than ever before.

The dulling of our senses is a recent phenomenon. In the not-so-distant past, we humans were intimately involved in the sensual world. The business of living required us to be physically immersed in nature to obtain food, clothing, shelter, even entertainment—and our senses had developed to fulfill these particular survival needs. Color vision helped us find ripe fruits; we never needed to develop infrared vision because we weren't nocturnal. Since we didn't fly, echolocation and sonar were not necessary, but our broad-spectrum hearing was. The "reality" our senses

show us is a narrow, selective slice of what's going on in the world around us, but it is all we required in the past for species survival. Today, our lifestyles are far removed from the natural, sensual world that spawned these senses, wrapped as we are in sterile buildings, synthetic materials, and artificial lighting. The pace and business of modern life diminishes our naturally vibrant senses.

To see how modern life differs from the sensual way humans have always lived, let's compare life now to the way it was during most of human history.

Food

We used to pluck tender berries and fruits, plunge into cold waters for fish and seafood, grind kernels of grain into flour, stalk the bush for prey, and gather fuels such as wood, peat, coal, and dried manure to feed the fire that gave us heat for our homes and cooking. Getting food was a primary and respected task of life, and eating was a communal event.

Now, we are propelled to the store in a car. Grocery shopping is low on our list of enjoyable tasks. We walk down brightly-lit aisles to choose all the items we need in one stop. Our foods are already prepared for us; bread has been baked, animals have been butchered, vegetables have been grown, picked, and frozen; even entire dinners have been cooked and packaged for us. At home, when it is time to cook, we turn a dial for instant, sustained heat. Preparing and eating meals is often a nuisance in our schedules.

Clothing

In the past, animals—provided we could find, catch, and kill them—provided us furs, skins, and sinews for making clothing. We'd scrape, ply, and chew the skins to make them usable, or raise sheep and goats to spin their wool into yarn and weave it into garments. Clothing ourselves took a lot of creativity, energy, and the involvement of all our senses.

Today, we look through a magazine, pick up the phone, and order a ready-made garment. We may walk through a climate-controlled mall to browse shops that hold every size and style of clothing we could want, and simply choose one to purchase and take home.

Shelter

Housing ourselves required a great involvement with materials; we'd cut trees, saw them into specific lengths, and construct dwellings. In some locations we'd stretch skins over frameworks of saplings, or make cubes of peat, ice, or clay to construct a shelter. Today, we sign some papers and within months a house appears, built by contractors with little involvement by us in the actual construction.

Work and Play

Anthropologists tell us that as hunters and gatherers, people worked far fewer hours per day than we do now. The rest of the time was spent on activities not essential to survival, but very central to a sensual, vibrant life. Cultures developed elaborate and

colorful celebrations, dances, music, and food. People spent much time fashioning masks and costumes, or creating musical instruments. Singing and storytelling were mainstay activities, as were games of chance and physical prowess. For millions of years of human history, humans worked only enough to ensure survival, and spent the rest of time in leisure and play to ensure happiness.

Certainly we modern people work. And work. First, we work at jobs that require at least forty hours per week, plus the time it takes to commute. More than half of us volunteer for charitable organizations. Then we have our regularly scheduled activities such as exercise, classes, rehearsals, or church groups. Children require shuttling from activity to activity. We have houses to maintain, both inside and out. We awaken to alarms, drive to work at sixty-five miles per hour or more, count heartbeats when we work out, and check our watches constantly throughout the day. In short, we live busy and fast-paced lives. We may even forget to play.

When we do allow ourselves leisure time, we have more entertainment options than ever from which to choose. But they are decidedly passive. They generally stimulate vision and hearing, but require no output or involvement by us. The daily ritual of sitting on the porch or around the fire, watching the sunset, or talking with a neighbor while listening to frogs croaking is replaced by staring at TV sitcoms. Instead of playing games of physical skill, we watch professional sports. Instead of making our own music, we turn a dial and get perfectly-engineered music produced in a studio. Instead of telling and acting out stories, we rent a video and watch it passively (and passive it is: the brain is less active when we watch television than when we sleep!). We

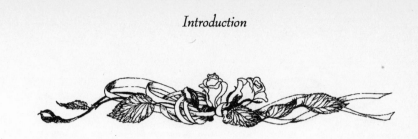

have an increasing onslaught of visual and aural stimuli, but it is mostly planned and packaged for us. It seduces us into passivity rather than encourages creativity and involvement.

This kind of living is killing sensuality. It's very easy to be passive, to accept the non-sensual in our lives. However, to live fully and sensually in this modern climate we don't have to go back to the wild and reject our entire lifestyle. We can regain our vibrant senses by increasing awareness of them and intentionally practicing sensual ways of living.

— Benefits of a Sensuous Life —

Living in accord with your senses will increase your peace. Whether you attribute sensation to a divine creative force or choose to view it as a purely biological function, you will experience a moment of peace each time you tune in to a stimulus. The momentary awareness of a sense raises you above the deadening cares and distractions of daily life. In lives regimented by day planners and tight schedules, we close down awareness of our senses and filter out a vast array of sensation. The drive to the office can become rich with intentional awareness of color. You can enjoy a business meeting more by appreciating the smell, heat, and sound of your coffee—which, amazingly, may help you remember more completely what was said. Larger, lasting peace comes with the gradual weaving in of sensual awareness to all aspects of your life. You may choose to spend more time in nature,

sitting quietly, or valuing more highly an interaction with a loved one. The more you notice and appreciate the bouquet of pleasures that surround you, the calmer and more peaceful you'll become.

Your life will also become more interesting. Since all you experience comes through your senses, the more you expand their capabilities, the more you will be able to experience in each moment. Sensuality leads you to explore, try new things, experiment, open your mind. You find new experiences all around you, and you get more out of them than ever before. By intentionally involving your senses, you also create more vivid, lasting memories. Life becomes more interesting to you, and you become more interesting to others.

Living sensually will help you regain a sense of wonder. As a child you sensed it; holding a lady bug, rubbing bare feet on the carpet, or finding an agate could transport you to awe. As adults we forget that joy exists primarily in simple, everyday moments. Adults think really wonderful experiences are far away and cost money, when true wonder pulses as close as the smoothness of someone's skin or the tang of raspberry juice. You will rediscover wonder in simple, available pleasures: the patterns of rain trickling down window glass, or the faint sizzling of pancakes cooking. Delight does not have to wait for the annual vacation to Mazatlán. Wonder lies all around you, and your senses provide constant access to it.

— What is a Sensual Person? —

A friend's dishwasher broke down and required costly repair. He never fixed it because washing dishes by hand was so pleasurable. He grew to appreciate the heat of the water, the crinkling sound of popping suds, the glaze of water on plates, and the lemony scent of the soap. Sensual awareness turned a typically undesirable task into daily pleasure. A co-worker confessed one day that she purposely minces garlic by hand so that she can smell the fragrance on her skin for hours. With a little practice, everyone can make sensuality an unconscious habit.

What is a sensual person like? A sensual person:

- Deliberately savors the taste of every food and drink
- Enjoys discovering smells of everything encountered
- Delights in touching various objects, feeling different textures and changes in temperature
- Listens for even the soft, unnoticed sounds
- Sees life through the eyes of an artist, appreciating light, dark, color, shape, and illusion
- Experiments with the senses
- Enjoys life, even in mundane tasks, because of an awareness and acceptance of sensual stimuli

— Keys to Sensual Enjoyment —

There are three keys to becoming this kind of joyful person: believing you deserve pleasure, following impulses, and living in a relaxed and healthful state.

Believe You Deserve Pleasure

Sensory enjoyment is a birthright. Every person is endowed with senses as their only means to experience and know the world. Even though Helen Keller was born deaf and blind, her sense of touch bridged her gap with others, allowing her to communicate with people and learn about the world. How fortunate you are to be reading this page, hearing background sounds, feeling the weight of the book in your hands. Your senses are little short of miraculous, and should be regarded with awe. Our ears magnify sound 200 times, and our brains constantly merge each eye's different view into one smooth scene. Reveling in your senses shows proper gratitude for the gift. Some people are uncomfortable seeking and accepting pleasure, perhaps due to a rigid upbringing where pleasure was considered frivolous or unholy. To truly enjoy the world your senses bring, you must believe that sensual living is a celebration of life. It is the art of finding beauty and holiness in simple things. We all deserve that.

Follow Impulses

Every day we squelch hundreds of tiny desires before they even reach our consciousness. So effective is this filter we rarely notice the desire to go barefoot, roll down a hillside, smell our slice of bread, or listen to bathwater. The activites in this book provide moments to increase your sensory input and leap the filter. Once you break your unconscious rules, it is that much easier to bypass them again, until you become totally aware of sensual opportunities. When you recognize even a glimmer of an impulse, follow it. If you want to touch that rough stone building, touch it! If you wonder what the dog food tastes like, nibble it! If your lover's stomach gurgles, put an ear to it and listen! Even if you feel a little silly, enjoy the tremulous feeling and follow your curiosity anyway. Eventually you'll discover that rarely does anyone truly care if you do something out of the ordinary.

Living sensually requires putting aside your "action editor" and engaging in life fully, as children do. Indulge your curiosity; you'll discover sounds that make you laugh, textures that delight you, sights that absorb you, and smells that stir memories.

One friend did just such a thing while running on mountain trails near Lake Tahoe. Entranced by the pure air, moist forest smell, unfamiliar footing, and sheer beauty of the primitive land, he had an irresistible urge to take his clothes off. It was an urge not for public display, but for enhancing the already sensual experience. He reveled in the exhilarating freedom and the wind blowing unbroken along his body—until he had to duck into bushes to

avoid hikers around the bend! Whether an action is "acceptable," like taking a new route home from work, or unusual, like my friend's, allow yourself to notice and follow impulses.

Relax and Live Healthfully

Stress in mind and body reduces the effectiveness of almost all the senses, as you'll discover in subsequent chapters. The musician who loses her "ear" when nervous, the athlete who misses the tie-breaking free throw, and the saleswoman whose eyes blur by the end of a long day all know how too much stress reduces their effectiveness. Mental stress equals body stress; there is no separation. Since the senses involve some of the body's most delicate and oxygen-dependent organs, they are among the first to be affected when stress constricts blood vessels. Relax often and release yourself from the rat race and productivity trap. Being stress-free allows the richness of your senses to come through so that you can enjoy life more.

The physical nature of our senses makes them susceptible not only to stress, but to other unhealthy lifestyle choices. Poor eating and exercise habits, smoking, drinking, and drug use all diminish the acuity of our senses. For example, hearing loss is associated with a high-fat diet; smoking damages the eye from both the inside and outside; a high-salt diet perpetuates itself by causing taste buds to require higher and higher amounts of salt to get the same taste. People who exercise regularly keep oxygen-rich blood supplied to their sensory organs, maximizing sensual capacity. The natural release of the body's "feel-good" drugs,

endorphins, gives the active person a natural high. Living sensually does not require one to be a competitive-level athlete or to
eliminate beer forever. It does require a love and respect of the
body as the self, and as the only means of thinking, feeling, and
experiencing. A healthy lifestyle will follow.

Let's begin this sensual journey.

1

Smell:
The Primeval Sense

The candle flame releases a pungent flicker of smoke. My nostrils instinctively flare to catch the scent—an ancient response warning me of danger. The smoke trails away, and as the candle settles into burning, it releases the fruity smell of raspberry scented wax. The scent overpowers the sterile machinery smell of my computer, making the writing of this chapter more pleasant.

All this smelling goes on at an almost subconscious level; we humans are least attentive to our olfactory sense. Yet it is our most ancient sense, and is most closely linked to our memory and emotions. Even though we are not consciously attuned to it, our sense of smell has amazing power in our lives. From playing a part in our selection of friends and lovers to

helping us diagnose diseases, smell is both a primitive and sophisticated sense.

— Why Is It so "Primitive"? —

Our sense of smell is the only sense that directly contacts the brain. Other senses are processed through the cognitive, or thinking, part of the brain. But smell is linked directly to the central and most ancient part of our brain, the limbic system (which was originally termed the "smell brain"). This area governs emotions, moods, motivation, and sexual behavior, and can be directly stimulated through the sense of smell.

As we breathe, we draw air over an area of yellow tissue high in the back of our nose. The area is the size of a quarter, and is covered with mucus. This patch of tissue contains 12 million specialized cells, each sporting ten to twenty hairlike growths called cilia. Each cilium has a receptor that can bind with an odor molecule.

When an odor molecule binds with one of our receptors, a nerve impulse travels through a hole in the skull to the olfactory bulb, located in that primeval center of the brain. Our brain then interprets the impulse to make us recognize "fish" or "grapefruit." The scent we register depends upon the combination of receptor cells that were stimulated. The various combinations allow us to detect over 10,000 different smells.

As a child, I would go ranging in large fields with the family black labrador, Tina. As I trotted steadily along, imagining I was on a horse, I would notice how Tina's path was erratic; she was

drawn to hundreds of places as if a string were attached to her nose. One day I decided to try to smell all she was smelling; on hands and knees I put my nose close to every spot she had sniffed. I smelled the same thing—a general earth and plants scent—all over. She obviously was in a higher realm of sensing. Some smells made her tail whip excitedly, some caused her to dig, some prompted her to shy back and avoid the spot altogether.

That was my first dawning of the gulf in olfaction between people and animals. Later I learned that while my receptor cells cover about four square centimeters, a dog's can be as big as 150 square centimeters.

Smell is a very direct sense, unlike sight or hearing. When we see something, we are really seeing light reflections. When we hear a sound, we are interpreting waves passing through the air. But our sense of smell is a physical interaction with the object we are smelling, since odor is caused by actual molecules of a substance being released. For example, bloodhounds are able to track people because each day we shed 50 million skin cells that form a physical trail wherever we go. Of course, the breed's 4 billion olfactory receptor cells certainly help.

— Smell and Food —

As anyone with a plugged nose can confirm, smell is highly integrated with taste. Our tongue alone can only sense four tastes: salty, sweet, bitter, and sour. It is our sense of smell that allows us the myriad variations of flavor. In fact, it is estimated that our sense of smell is 10,000 times more developed than our sense of

taste. We smell food before we eat it, but we also smell it after we've put it in our mouth; molecules travel up the passage called the pharynx, which connects the back of the mouth to the nose. This enhances the taste of food. One cook I know uses smell, not taste, to determine what seasonings to add to a dish. His finely developed sense of smell guides him more surely than a taste test.

Many animals rely primarily on smell to find food. The snake gathers scent particles from the air on its forked tongue, and tastes them on a special organ at the back of its mouth. I have seen a spot where a wolf clawed through four inches of ice to get a beaver carcass she'd smelled. Mosquitoes are attracted to their feast by the scent of carbon dioxide we emit as we exhale. Polar bears can smell a dead seal from over twelve miles away.

You've probably noticed the connection yourself. Perhaps the aroma from a nearby bakery makes you salivate, or walking into a house where soup is cooking suddenly makes you feel hungry. Smell increases saliva and stimulates the digestive tract, making metabolism of food more efficient. Certainly smell is an element in the enjoyment of eating.

— Haven't I Smelled You Here Before? —

You have a personal scent, as individual as your fingerprint. This odor affects people around you, even when they don't consciously smell it. Have you ever noticed that people's homes have different

smells? While some of the scents are created from paint, cleaning products, and carpeting, many are created by the people living in the home. Even individual bedrooms will have a distinct scent based on the inhabitant. I often notice that when I open my clothes closet I detect the familiar scent of myself.

In a survey of 800 American women by Quest International, smell ranked fourth highest in personal attributes women notice when first meeting someone. Face, eyes, and voice ranked above smell, but hair, dress, skin, and hands ranked lower.

This recognition of individual human scents is well documented. In one study, people were given three identical T-shirts. Three-fourths of the people studied could pick out the one they had worn. In another experiment, mothers were given identical baby clothes, and most could pick out the clothes their own baby had been wearing. The mother/infant scent bond goes the other way as well; studies of infant olfaction show that a ten-day-old infant can detect and identify the smell of her mother's breasts. The baby will turn toward the mother's smell, and away from the smell of any other mother.

Where does this scent come from? Sweat, for one thing. We have scent-producing apocrine glands in all the places we sweat—armpits, genitals, anus, and even our face. Hair concentrated in these areas harbors the bacteria necessary for scent production; the bacteria react with the apocrine secretions to form our distinctive body odor. However, people around the world vary; those of African descent may have glands on their chests and near their

navels, Australian aborigines have scent glands in front of their ears, while Japanese people have no sweat glands under their arms. Until recently, body odor was sufficient reason to be discharged from the Imperial Japanese Army because anyone with a body odor was considered to have an abnormal condition.

Diet also influences our body smell, as an American friend discovered while traveling in China. Due to her comparatively fatty and meat-laden diet, she smelled offensive to the primarily vegetarian Chinese. The food we eat, the spices we use, even the mode of cooking will all affect our natural scent. People who eat Indian food have an exotic dark smell; those who feast on Italian have a scent laced with garlic. When we are surrounded by people who eat a similar diet, we don't notice the difference; our nose perks up when a different smell arrives on the scene.

Many people are repulsed by the idea of sweat and "body odor." But these smells exist even on the cleanest of bodies. They are natural, desirable, and even necessary. These glands switch on at puberty, off at menopause, and in between play a large role in our attraction to others.

After puberty, the glands emit hormones called androstenal and androsterone, from here on referred to as "pheromones," a word used to describe a substance that is produced by a male or female and elicits a response from the same species. Pheromones allow both children and adults to distinguish between the genders purely by smell, however unconsciously. Animals rely on pheromones for marking territory. Cats seem to affectionately rub their faces against you; they are marking you as theirs with scent from glands on their cheeks. Dogs have a well-known method of

depositing scent markers. Deer leave scent trails from glands on their legs, while Thompson's gazelles deposit a substance secreted beneath their eyes on twigs and grass. Ants leave a chemical trail for others to stake out food routes, which is why you often see them traveling in single file to and from your sugar bin. Ocean salmon rely on scent cues to locate their natal stream five years after they hatch.

Mating animals have magnificent powers of scent production and detection. When a female emperor moth exudes her sexual perfume, a male can detect her from three miles away. In many mammals, urine indicates the sexual state of the female. Goldfish can detect one gram of their sexual pheromone in 40 billion gallons of water, equivalent to 10,000 Olympic swimming pools. Studies of human pheromones prove the significance of their effects on us as well. In one study, the male pheromone androsterone was sprayed on seats in a dentist's waiting room. Women consistently chose those seats more than men did. Another experimenter showed men photographs of women. Photos sprayed with androstenol were consistently rated more attractive than those with no scent added.

It should be no surprise, then, that people kiss. Glands around our mouths produce a pheromone, which is also found in saliva. In some cultures, the word for "kiss" means "smell," presumably in recognition of the pleasure of drinking in someone's personal scent. One-fourth of the people who lose their sense of smell lose their sex drive as well, according to Robert Henkin from the Center for Sensory Disorders at Georgetown University.

Our body scents used to be more highly valued; it was not until the nineteenth century that we developed attitudes that body odor was undesirable. Napoleon wrote to Josephine requesting her not to wash because he was coming home soon. In Elizabethan times sweethearts would exchange "love apples"; a woman would keep a peeled apple in her armpit until it was saturated with her sweat, then give it to her lover to inhale. Body smells were strong and quite accepted, as bathing was considered something to be done infrequently. The valerian plant was considered a pleasant perfume, so much so that it was used to scent clothing. By our modern standards, however, valerian has a penetrating "goaty" or sweaty smell.

Our pheromones don't just affect the opposite sex. In observing women who lived in a dormitory, psychologist Martha McClintock discovered that women who live or spend a lot of time together develop the same menstrual cycles. Studies since found that when the sweat of a woman is repeatedly daubed under the noses of other women, those women's menstrual patterns will synchronize with the donor's within three to four months. Women in a control group who had alcohol daubed under the nose experienced no change in their cycles.

Changes in emotional states change the type of pheromone we emit. Dogs, horses, and cats can tell when you're afraid because you emit a different combination of scents when stressed. But you're not alone; impalas warn the rest of the herd of danger by kicking a chemical trail into the air from scent glands on their rear feet.

Because of our modern cleanliness fetish, we scrub away all traces of natural odors, then replace them with perfumes and

colognes, made, ironically, from the sex smells of animals and plants. Perfumes are made with musk from the ventral pouches of Himalayan musk deer, castoreum from the beaver's anal gland, civet from the anal sacs of African cats, and oil from the pistil and stamens of flowers. There is now a product on the market that contains human pheromones, for use in attracting the opposite sex. Little do the consumers realize that simply allowing their own pheromones to surround them would accomplish the same objective.

— Happy Smell, Sad Smell —

Since olfaction takes place in the part of the brain that is considered the seat of the emotions, it is little wonder that smell, more than any other sense, affects our emotions and moods. Certainly we react when we smell smoke in the house; our body immediately releases adrenaline and other hormones to prepare us for action. A whiff of spoiled food causes us to recoil from the danger of potential food poisoning.

In contrast, scents can also calm us. The ancient form of herbal medicine, aromatherapy, is based upon the idea that the distilled essence, or essential oils, of flowers, herbs, and plants can make people feel better both physically and psychologically. Aromatherapists use the smell of geranium to reduce stress, and the scent of rose to lift depression. Modern studies have shown that the smell of vanilla helps patients relax when undergoing the often claustrophobic magnetic resonance imaging (MRI) test.

Scents affect our emotions and moods by affecting our brain waves. Jasmine speeds up brain waves and acts as a stimulant, while lavender slows them down and works as a sedative.

The actual physical effect of the smell causes a change in our emotive state. Sometimes, however, it may be purely our connotation of a smell that changes our mood. Even Scrooge's emotions were tweaked by smell: "He was conscious of a thousand odors floating in the air, each one connected with a thousand thoughts, and hopes, and joys, and cares long, long forgotten," wrote Charles Dickens in *A Christmas Carol*. Odors send signals racing straight from the olfactory bulbs to the limbic system, seat of the emotions, and the hippocampus, which controls memory. The smell of PlayDoh gives me happy childhood memories, but to a man whose mother died the day he was playing with PlayDoh, the smell produces anxiety.

Scents can spark memories and moods years after an event. In the words of Rudyard Kipling, "Smells are surer than sounds or sights to make your heartstrings crack." The novelist Marcel Proust dipped a madeleine biscuit into his tea and the aroma triggered a flood of beautiful childhood memories, forming the basis of his multi-volume *A là Recherche du Temps Perdu (Remembrance of Things Past)*. I remember a trip down California's Highway 1 almost entirely by the intense smells I experienced: eucalyptus leaves, lemon grass, ocean surf, and the delicious pulp scent of prickly pear fruit.

Not every scent will have the same connotations for each person. However, psychiatrist J. R. King has found that sea fra-

grance has the most universally positive connotation as could be found. He uses the fragrance during deep relaxation therapy.

Smells can relax us, but tests have also shown that smell can improve our alertness. A University of Cincinnati study had subjects perform a forty-minute test in which they were to watch a video screen and press a button whenever a certain line pattern appeared. Subjects who were given whiffs of peppermint and lily-of-the-valley performed better than subjects who were given unscented air.

In Japan, thirteen keypunch operators were monitored eight hours a day for a month. When the air was scented with lavender, errors per hour dropped 21 percent. When jasmine was used, errors dropped 33 percent, and with the scent of lemon errors dropped 54 percent. The use of smells to enhance efficiency and reduce stress is becoming common in Japan, where various fragrances are delivered through air-conditioning ducts.

Some stores infuse the air with scents that stimulate people to buy more, and casinos may soon waft scent through the gaming areas, as certain aromas encourage people to gamble more.

Personality also plays a role in how scents affect our emotions. German perfumers use color rosettes to help people select fragrances, having found that color and odor preference are linked—and personality determines both. Extroverts prefer fresh fragrances; introverts tend toward oriental scents. Emotionally ambivalent people usually choose floral scents, and emotionally steady people tend to have no particular preference.

— Medicinal Smell —

Aromatherapy has been used since ancient times to treat illnesses of all kinds. As early as 5,000 years ago, the Egyptians used cedarwood oil in cosmetics and the mummification process, perhaps understanding the natural preservative effect. Infused oils and unguents were employed for both spiritual and medicinal purposes, relieving and healing skin inflammations. The essential oils of certain plants produced physical effects on people, leading to a compendium of knowledge of nature's olfactory pharmacy. The scent of lavender is used to heal wounds and burns, and with the more recent determination that lavender slows the brain waves and acts as a relaxant, one can see how healing would be enhanced. Juniper combats sluggish digestion and fatigue, while eucalyptus relieves flu symptoms, sinus pains, laryngitis, asthma, and rheumatism. Even mainstream products like eucalyptus cough drops, Vick's VapoRub and Ben Gay ointment use aromatherapy properties to physically benefit us. Many essences are used for their hygienic properties because they naturally retard the growth of bacteria, fungus, and yeast.

While scents have long been used in the treatment of illness, the sense of smell also helps diagnose disease. At one time, people thought bad odors caused disease such as malaria—the word comes from the Italian words *mala aria,* or "bad air"—and Italians believed exhalations from marshes in the neighborhood of Rome caused the illness.

Though that theory died when scientists discovered that mosquitoes spread the disease, other smells associated with disease

continue to have validity in diagnosis. Certain diseases cause metabolic by-products or bacterial decomposition which produce certain smells in people. People suffering from diabetes develop an acetone smell on their breath. Yellow fever produces a butcher shop smell, typhoid causes a smell like fresh-baked brown bread, and diabetic coma makes someone smell fruity. Other diseases spawn smells like stale beer and maple syrup. The University of Pennsylvania Smell and Taste Center found that patients with Alzheimer's and Parkinson's diseases suffer identical smell loss, and this can be used as a clue to early detection.

— Improve Your Sniffer —

After a glimpse into how significant your sense of smell is, the next step is to improve it to make your life experience more rich. Following are ways you can remove barriers that dull olfaction.

Quit Smoking and Avoid Smoke-filled Places

People who smoke or have previously smoked have a lowered ability to smell. The good news is that the effect is reversible; olfaction improves the longer a person stops exposure to tobacco smoke. Researchers are not yet clear on exactly how smoking adversely affects olfaction; it is likely that the chemicals in smoke damage the mucous and olfactory cells. Second-hand smoke is

increasingly implicated in the same health problems that smokers experience, so to keep your sense of smell clear and sensitive, steer away from smoke altogether.

Eliminate Overkill

One day I noticed that I used honey-scented shampoo, lemon-scented conditioner, and perfumed soap in the shower. When I stepped out, I applied talcum with "powder fresh scent." Then I moisturized my face with a perfumed cream. On my body I used an aloe lotion that was heavily scented. Then I brushed my teeth with mint toothpaste, and spritzed on a bit of hair spray that smelled like apples. The jeans and shirt I donned had been washed in scented laundry detergent and dried with a strong-smelling softener sheet. By the time I finished getting ready I smelled like a chemical factory. Had I then added cologne, my house might have exploded.

My point is this: avoid artificially-scented products. We use so many products that our bodies and homes become infused with an amalgam of contrived fragrances. This chemical overkill tires and deadens our sense of smell, causing us to miss the subtle scents of natural things. Synthetic fragrances, even those that seem to smell exactly like what they are imitating, are often manufactured from petroleum by-products and can be harsh to our delicate olfactory and body tissues. Many people are irritated by the heavy perfumes used in detergents, cleaning products, and toiletries. Unscented and non-allergenic products can eliminate

the reaction. It is becoming increasingly common for cities and states to declare "scent-free" zones in some public places so that people can avoid being assaulted by artificial scents on others.

Buying unscented products also allows you the control to select only the most pleasing scents in your life. I usually choose to add no scent to my body or house, as I like the warm scent I produce naturally. Others may have a favorite aftershave or perfume, and avoiding the overkill of perfumed products allows the true essence of that scent to come through.

Take a Clue from Canines

When trying to smell something, especially if it is faint, imagine a dog. Dogs will face the wind, if there is one. They will hold perfectly still to eliminate distraction. Their noses will tilt upward to receive the scent most directly. The nostrils will flare, again to increase the chance of catching those molecules of scent. They will slowly move their heads around to find the place they catch the strongest odor. The wetness of their noses allows particles to dissolve and thus be smelled. And finally, they will be patient, allowing time to concentrate on even faint whiffs.

You can use these same techniques. When outdoors, periodically face the wind and smell what comes along. And any time, reposition your head to experience the most of that scent. If the odor is in front of you, it helps to tilt your nose upward a bit, since nostrils open downward. Your nostrils automatically flare at times when you smell something good; use that option intentionally as

well, to increase the amount of the air you take in, and thus the amount of scent particles. If the air is humid, scent molecules will be dissolved and easy to smell. To increase your smell acuity on dry days, wet the inside of your nose.

Practice Sniffing

Your olfactory cells die and new ones grow every thirty to ninety days. Tests have shown that you can improve your sensing of certain smells by repeatedly smelling them; scientists theorize that stimulating the olfactory receptors may cause them to multiply.

— Let's Practice! —

The purpose of these activities is to increase your awareness of smell, so that you start noticing and appreciating this sense. Once I became tuned in to smell, I started noticing subtleties I had always missed, such as certain smells associated with playing my violin. The faint musty smell of old wood, the machine scent of the metal-wound strings, and the occasional whiff of rosin dust now all signify part of my musical experience.

"Picture" Smells

If I asked you to think of the color blue, you could probably see the color in your mind. But if I ask you to think of the smell of a library, you probably can't draw up the smell. This may be because smell does not pass through our cognitive brain—it is more experiential than intellectual. However, trying to "picture" smells can help increase your awareness. It can also spark memories that are linked with these smells.

The exercise is simple: think of each of the following smells, one by one. Allow yourself at least thirty seconds on each one. Closing your eyes can help bring the scent to mind. Breathe in through your nose, as if the smell were all around you. Allow the memory to grow to the point that you actually smell the scent.

- Lake air
- Apples
- Newspaper
- Manure
- Tool box
- Strawberries
- Baby powder
- Tar
- Lilacs
- Lemons
- Natural gas
- Skunk

- Carnations
- Anise
- Bread baking
- Air after a rain
- Freshly mowed grass
- Cloves
- Popcorn at the theater
- Mint

The Kitchen Game

This is fun to do with a few friends as a way to exercise the sense of smell. Gather ten items from the kitchen that would have a familiar scent to people in the group. Examples are raisins, peanut butter, cinnamon, lettuce (let cold items warm to room temperature), oranges, coffee grounds, pepper, graham crackers, apples, and cheese.

Have each person number a sheet of paper from one to ten, and then blindfold each player.

Hold the first item under each player's nose until the person has smelled his or her fill. Make sure you tell the group not to say what they think the item is. After everyone has smelled the item, tell them to write what they think the object is next to number one on their sheet of paper. Do this for each item you have chosen from the kitchen. At the end, tell them what each item was and see how many they identified correctly.

People will find the smells familiar but often be unable to accurately name them. They may mistake the smell of raisins for

brown sugar, or cinnamon for cloves. When you reveal the answers, people will immediately wonder how they could not have correctly named the items they missed.

This is great for making us realize how much we rely on vision to identify things, when most foods and many other items can be distinguished by smell just as easily—if only we are tuned to it.

Nose Plug

The next time you are eating something, plug your nose before you've had a chance to smell the food item. Not only will you not smell it before you put it into your mouth, you'll also miss the waft of scent that normally travels up the back passage from your mouth to your nose. You'll be amazed at how a piece of toast, for example, tastes about as interesting as cardboard, or how tuna fish could just as well be rubber. When you unplug your nose you'll fully appreciate the richness that olfaction lends to eating.

Skin Scent

Right now, smell the back of your hand. Put your nose right on it. If the smell is not obscured by scented soap or lotion, you will get a very faint, warm skin scent. Keep smelling it, drawing air slowly into your nose. It is almost a non-smell, it is so subtle. But it is pleasing.

If you are reading this book during a warm season, go outside in the sun in a short-sleeved shirt, and let your skin be heated
for at least fifteen minutes. Then smell it again. Now it will have a
more tangy scent.

Nearly half the adult population cannot smell androsterone,
one of the human pheromones found in perspiration. However,
scientists have found that 50 percent of those people can develop
the ability to smell it by sniffing it daily. Researchers hypothesize
that stimulating certain smell receptors causes them to multiply.

Therefore, even if you do this exercise and are convinced you
smell nothing, keep on sniffing. You will develop a higher sensitivity to human scent. Smell other peoples' skin—preferably of
people you know well. Baby skin has a peaceful smell; men's skin
has a slightly musky smell; sweaty skin has a zing to it. Learn to
appreciate natural human odor.

Nature Walk

You can do this even in a city park, but for a real treat get out of
the city and into nature. Then, simply be a sensual explorer.
Crush a leaf in your hand and draw in its "green" scent. Get on
hands and knees and put your nose right next to the earth for the
rich organic smell. Put some pine tree sap on your finger and
smell the spice throughout the day. Smell the breeze coming off a
body of water. You may develop to the point that you can smell
animals; with conditions right, I have smelled deer before I saw
them, and some hunters use the musky scent of deer and elk to
help locate their prey.

In Melbourne, Australia, the Royal Botanical Gardens features an herb garden. Each herb is labeled for its purpose, such as medicinal, edible, or aromatic. Visitors are encouraged to rub their fingers on a leaf of any herb they wish to get the lovely fragrance. I ended up with ten fingers of different scents, which I individually smelled and enjoyed for the several hours they lasted. This memorable experience taught me to relish scents of nature everywhere I go.

Comparisons

Upon smelling some blue-red roses I exclaimed, "These smell like apples." A scoffer came over, smelled them, and pronounced, "No, they smell exactly like roses." So we did a test. She closed her eyes, and I held half an apple under her nose. She had to guess if it was an apple, or a rose. Even with a 50-50 chance, she incorrectly guessed it was a rose. Dark roses really do smell like apples.

Another time I was picking raspberries and took warning, because I smelled skunk. I looked carefully around, and saw no skunk. Back I went to the berry bush, and sure enough, there was that scent again. It was then I noticed that I was crushing some onion plants under my feet. I couldn't believe I had mistaken the smell of onion for skunk, but upon closer sniffing of the plants, it was clear they were the source. Of course, once I knew the smell belonged to onions, it no longer smelled like skunk to me. My brain had categorized it differently.

The point of these two stories is to show how many things have similar scents, yet our compartmentalizing brains may not allow us to draw the comparisons. Onions cooking can smell just like body odor, but we don't like body odor, and we do like onions.

Try thinking, "what does this smell like?" when you are savoring a smell. When you let go of your boundaries you may discover that lettuce and grapefruit have a similar fragrance, or that carnations and fresh broccoli smell very much alike.

Savoring Food Scents

Why not get more enjoyment out of the same amount of food? Sensual people make a habit of savoring its smell as well as its taste. Think of food as something to be smelled as well as eaten, and you get double the sensory experience.

At your next meal or snack, spend at least ten seconds simply smelling a food before you eat it. Allow the rich smell of lasagna to fill your nose. Enjoy the yeasty smell of bread. Let the scent of orange juice tickle you. Draw in the comforting aroma of tea.

At home you can unabashedly lean down close to your plate, close your eyes and breathe in deeply, and I encourage this. In the employee dining room, however, that may not go over well. You can still commit to enjoying the smell of food everywhere; in public you can be more subtle by pausing when you bring a bite of food to your mouth, and inhaling through your nose. I occasionally get "caught" smelling the fragrant wrapper of a piece of gum or chocolate candy, but take it as an opportunity to share a delicious smell with someone.

Come back to these exercises occasionally to remind yourself to use your sense of smell. It is proven that smell thresholds can be lowered with training. Not only will you get more enjoyment out of this often-overlooked sense, but you'll actually improve it.

2

Touch:
The Essential Sense

I am lying face-down next to a saltwater pool in Kuranda, a small town in the jungle of northern Queensland, Australia. My eyes are closed, the soporific heat lulling me into a blissful doze. The thick humidity muffles sounds and quiets even the birds, also taking a siesta. I have absorbed the rich tropical smell so long that my nose is sated. Right now, my body has only one grand sensation: touch.

Bare stomach and thighs pressing into the rough concrete deck tingle from the riddling of tiny, jutting pebbles. The skin on my back and arms glows with the sun's heat as it penetrates my inner body. As the salt water evaporates, my skin pulls one size too tight. I feel the secure gravity of my weight rooting me down. The swimsuit draws a firm line into my buttocks. I notice the muscles in my face relax and droop, and the thunking of my heart slow down. I feel good. I feel.

Touch is the all-over sense. We are totally encased in our primary touch organ, the skin, and we have touch receptors located throughout our bodies in muscles and joints. We can sense the outer world, as in the softness of a cat's fur, and the inner world, like the churn of an empty stomach or bliss of a good bowel movement. Not only is touch our most pervasive sense, but it is our most attentive as well, even while we sleep. Upon awakening it is the first sense to recover fully. Touch is the first sense to develop in an embryo. A general law of embryology states that the earlier a function develops, the more fundamental it is likely to be. Certainly a person can go through life without sight, hearing, smell or taste, but no one can survive without the sense of touch and the functions performed by the skin.

— What is Skin? —

Weighing six to ten pounds, and stretching to two square yards, the skin is the largest organ of the body. It is composed of two layers: the thick, spongy underlayer called the dermis, and the thin upper layer, called the epidermis. The dermis is rich in elastic connective tissue and the protein collagen, and serves to protect and cushion the body. It holds hair follicles, nerve endings, sweat glands, and blood and lymph vessels. The epidermis is the part we see, and is composed of cells that have spent fifteen to thirty days

moving from a plump beginning near the dermis to the outer boundary of the body, where they are routinely sloughed off.

Skin has an enormous number of receptors sensitive to heat, cold, pressure, and pain. They are distributed unevenly, with some places such as lips, hands, and tongue having a higher concentration than places like the thigh or back. We also have the "proprioreceptive" sense, which is awareness of body movement, posture, and perception of weight. Sensors in our joints and tendons are stimulated primarily by movement and posture of the body. These provide sensory clues that permit precise movements. Well over half a million sensory fibers from the skin enter the spinal cord, and these are generally of larger size than those associated with other senses. The feedback from skin and internal receptors to brain is constant, even when we sleep, so that our body is in continuous adjustment to our environment (a major reason we change positions in our sleep is that skin pressed against the mattress becomes overheated).

Pigments (or lack of them) in the skin give us color. Skin defines the outer edge of our organism, our shape. It protects our underlying parts from injury, radiation, and invasion of foreign substances. It is a living wineskin holding in all our body fluids and keeping soft organs and muscles neatly in place. The Vitamin D it produces upon exposure to sunlight is essential to life. Skin heats and cools us, and is portable, washable, dustproof, self-mending, breathable, and waterproof (even though it is full of tiny holes). In other words, it's the perfect outerwear. Furthermore, at least until we are very old, it is always the right size. As we grow,

or gain and lose weight, our elastic skin will expand and rebound. Even after stretching thin and tight over a pregnant belly, skin can resume its former size in as little as six weeks.

The thickness of skin varies from 1/25-inch on eyelids to 1/8-inch or more on palms, soles, and between the shoulder blades. Places that are subject to rubbing or pressure genetically tend to be thicker; however, the skin also responds to various pressures by building up wherever needed. My left hand's hardened fingertips attest to years of playing violin and guitar. Gripping a pen every day has produced a round knob on my right hand's middle finger. My in-line skates press on the inside of each ankle, causing roughened spots.

Skin tissue comes in a wide variety of forms, including claws, spines, hooves, scales, feathers, nails, and hair. The human scalp sports 100,000 to 150,000 hairs, which, though we romanticize hair, are thin, dead shafts of cells growing out of specialized structures in the dermis called follicles. A hair grows about one centimeter a month for two to six years, then is shed along with fifty to 100 other hairs that fall each day. The human body has five million hairs; the only skin without hair covers the palms, soles of feet, lips, anus, and parts of the external genitals. Skin is thinner and more sensitive wherever there is hair.

I remember in grade school pulling an individual hair on the head of an unsuspecting classmate to see how much motion was needed for the person to react. I didn't know that at the base of the hair follicle is a nerve ending, and that touching the tip of a hair can be enough to vibrate it and spark that sensory nerve. Whiskers on cats, rats, and mice are so sensitive and central to the animal's

orientation that dewhiskering these creatures handicaps them more than the loss of sight or smell. The normally nimble cat will stumble and bump into things in the dark without its whiskers.

Fingernails, hooves, and claws are a specialized form of skin with a unique feature: they have a free edge that keeps growing. If you smash your finger in a drawer and get a white "bruise" at the base of your nail, it will be six to seven months before that mark reaches the edge. This edge needs cutting or wearing down to prevent disabling the hands. I remember pictures of the man with the world's longest fingernails; his fingers were rendered useless by the endless looping nails. Likewise, I have seen horses whose hooves had grown into upturned elf feet through lack of trimming or wear on hard surfaces. House dogs need their claws trimmed routinely to curb the constant growth that in nature is worn off on hard ground and rocks.

— Touch and Grow —

Many hospitals, like Children's Hospital of St. Paul, Minnesota, know that infants who are touched often cry less, sleep more, gain weight 50 percent faster, and have better temperaments than those who are touched less often. This hospital encourages "Kangaroo Care," where the premature infant rests skin to skin against the parent's bare chest. The baby absorbs the warmth, sight, odor, and movement, and the close contact forges the important bond between child and parent. Studies suggest that during this skin-to-skin contact, the parent stabilizes the baby's temperature

because the parent's temperature will rise or fall as needed to keep the baby warm. In addition, milk volume in mothers is increased. Infants receiving touch therapy tend to get out of incubators sooner.

Other hospitals have volunteers who massage preemies to encourage more active, alert, and responsive babies. Studies have shown that infants who were massaged for fifteen minutes, three times a day, showed signs of more rapidly maturing nervous systems than those not massaged. This was demonstrated by their increased responsiveness to things such as a face or a rattle. Eight months later, these infants did better in tests of mental and motor ability than did non-massaged infants.

Touch seems to be not only pleasant, but actually essential for proper human growth and development. We know it is true in the animal world; studies have proven this many times. Rat pups deprived of their mother's licking and grooming virtually stop growing. In a series of studies by H. Harlow and R. Zimmerman, baby monkeys raised in a wire mesh cage had difficulty surviving during the first five days of life. Those whose cages included a wire-mesh cone that they could cling to did better, and those with a cone that was covered with terrycloth grew into large, healthy babies. In a related experiment, baby monkeys were provided with two surrogate mothers: one constructed of wire mesh with nipples that provided milk, and one that provided no food but was made of terrycloth. Even though the wire mother gave them food, the babies spent most of their time clinging to the cloth mother.

Pregnant animals lick themselves extensively, which stimulates all their body functions and aids in the growth of mammary

glands. In experiments where no licking was allowed before birth, rats made poor mothers. They failed to build nests, moved away from pups that wanted to nurse, and had underdeveloped mammary glands. Other experiments have found that removing newborn young from a mother for as little as a half hour interrupts the natural bond and licking behavior; the quality of mothering is impaired even after the young is returned.

Even in the birth process we need touch; there are biological differences between vaginally born and Caesarean babies. The tight squeezing and stimulation of labor prepares all the baby's systems for functioning; it is thought that because humans don't lick their young, the extensive labor is necessary for triggering the baby's body systems necessary for after birth. Caesarean babies must be massaged and handled immediately to gain a similar effect. Even the age-old slap on the bottom is a rousing activity that starts a baby breathing.

The need for touch at birth goes both ways; the mother's uterus is stimulated to contract when the newborn nurses. These strong contractions force out any remaining clots and afterbirth, effectively cleaning the uterus as well as returning it to normal size. Breastfeeding has enormous positive biological effects on the mother. It stimulates a "mothering hormone" that actually enhances the mother's bond to her child. Breast milk, nature's perfect human baby food, is nutritionally superior to any supplement, and the act of breastfeeding best fills a baby's high need for touch.

In many cultures, children are constantly in contact with someone; in Bali, a baby spends the whole day slung on mother's

hip as she pounds rice. An Inuit baby, wearing just a caribou-skin diaper, rides on his mother's bare back; a thick fur parka covers both of them. The baby spends all his time in contact with the mother's skin, hearing her voice, feeling and hearing her heart-beat, bending and swaying with her as she goes about her day. The "undeveloped" world gives its babies constant contact; whether by a mother or a sister or a village aunt, babies in many cultures receive continual handling.

Western culture promotes quite the opposite. Our infants sleep in separate beds, usually in a separate room from parents. Cribs, playpens, swings, and strollers—not to mention clothes—keep our children separate from our bodies for almost all the day and certainly all the night. We commonly bottlefeed instead of the natural choice of breastfeeding, and even our breastfeeding is usually terminated within the first year. Our culture believes that a child can be "spoiled" by too much loving touch; we endorse a harsh "go it alone" paradigm and treat our children accordingly. It's then easy to see why thumb-sucking and blanket-holding are common in the Western world, but virtually non-existent in cultures where children receive sufficient skin stimulation.

— Touching the Emotions —

Besides being essential, touch just plain feels good. My young niece loves to take a lock of someone's hair and tickle her face with it, closing her eyes in pure bliss and smiling as she relishes the sensation. Cats and dogs nose their way onto laps to be petted and scratched. Snakes, lizards, and other cold-blooded creatures

bask in the sun to warm their bodies; we warm-bloodeds bask in the sun because the heat feels so delicious. Bears and horses will scratch against rough bark, and we love a backscratch even in the absence of an itch. An old proverb says, "'Tis better than riches to scratch where it itches." Birds enjoy a dust or water bath. Many animals roll in the sand, snow, water, grass, or mud.

As a child, I often had to be reminded not to touch certain things that felt irresistable, like the fox fur collar in front of me in church, or the thick swashes of oil paints sweeping across museum paintings. Children are extremely in tune with touch, until society trains it out of them. Youngsters relish touch-and-feel museums where they can finger deer antlers and coyote fur, or spookhouses where peeled grapes represent a dead man's eyes and cold spaghetti is said to be human intestines. For them, touch is good for touch's sake; wanting to know how something feels is reason enough to touch it.

People use pleasurable sensations to drive away negative moods. When you feel physically good, you tend to feel emotionally good. In many cultures, people finger a smooth stone or bead; the brain wave patterns induced by the pleasurable sensation of this "worry bead" help smooth away tension. Rosary beads may do the same, the repeated sensual stimulation driving away distraction. People also use self-touch to comfort themselves. We wring our hands, purse our lips, rub our palms together or smooth the top of our thighs as instinctive tension relievers. Unconsciously we may rub or press acupressure points that connect to the areas of our body undergoing stress.

We touch each other to feel good, too. Like animals, we enjoy having our hair brushed (a high concentration of touch

receptors exists wherever we have hair). Ancient Romans, Greeks, and Egyptians wore elaborate coifs that required the constant ministrations of hairdressers. People around the world know the pleasure of braiding each other's hair; they experience a sensual "high" when another person parts and tugs at their hair to plait it. Not only is the sensation sublime, but the intimacy of the act wraps the receiver in a warm blanket of security.

Unlike Mediterranean cultures, North Americans do not voluntarily crowd together at a bus stop, or ascribe to the close personal space common to Latin cultures. Ours is a distant society, where the dominant paradigm says touching someone of the same gender is taboo, and touching someone of the opposite sex is a sexual overture. I always notice with humor the constant shifting of bodies as people enter or leave an elevator; everyone tries to keep the maximum amount of space possible between each other. This no-touch culture has contributed to the high rate of pet ownership in the United States, especially of cats and dogs, animals that are highly touchable.

Massage has been used for centuries for healing and pleasure. It stimulates circulation, relaxes tense muscles, dilates blood vessels, and cleans toxins out of the body through the flow of lymph. Additionally, it helps provide our necessary emotional and biological quota of touch stimulation. There are many styles of massage. Swedish uses long, sweeping strokes in the direction of the heart, while "neo-Reichian," used in psychotherapy, dispels nervous energy using strokes away from the heart. Japanese shi-atsu follows the principles of acupuncture, touching the body according to meridians, or pathways of life force. Reflexology

attends to pressure points on the skin of hands and feet, which are connected to various organs of the body. Rolfing, a more extreme and deep manipulation of the body, is said to bring energies back into balance. Whatever the method, any loving stimulation of the skin feels good and brings physical benefits.

— The Sex Connection —

Of all the creatures on earth, humans are the most elaborate lovers. We enjoy sex as an emotional and physical pleasure far more often than as a procreative act. Aside from the one-time massive stimulation we experience as babies during the birth process, sex can be our most tactually involving experience, combining use of lips, tongue, hands, genitals, and virtually every surface area of our skin. In its best context it flows from a height of love, intimacy, and passion, involving us emotionally as well as physically.

As a testament to the pleasure of human sexuality, the female clitoris has no reproductive function—it is purely an organ of pleasure. Facial lips are well endowed with nerve endings, making kissing any part of someone's body a highly sensual experience (anthropologists have supposed that the facial lips have unconsciously come to represent vaginal lips, which become reddish, swollen, and wet during sexual excitement, which is why women redden their lips with lipstick and gloss them to shine). Limiting sexual pleasure to the genitals would be missing much of

the experience because the entire skin becomes a sexual organ. Some people feel "electricity" upon touching another, and it is true. Skin is a good conductor of electricity, as you may notice when you touch someone and feel a "shock." The psychogalvanometer, or lie detector, is one way of measuring skin electricity. Emotional changes cause the autonomic nervous system to produce an increase in the electrical conductance of the skin.

Sex for many people has been relegated to a solely physical act, and does not provide the zenith experience that is possible within a rich relationship. A series of motions does not constitute pleasure; a genital touch can be arousing, alarming, or dull, depending upon its context. Conversely, a simple touch on the hand can be an erotic event. A truly sensual sexual experience will include a high emotional involvement between the partners. Ancient Tantric love manuals and Chinese "pillow books" promote the loving emotional as well as physical involvement of the partners as the key to heightened sexual experience.

Various Native American tribes used a "courting blanket" that couples would publicly wrap around themselves, showing others that they were a couple and promoting physical closeness. North American culture has relegated the physical expression of affection to nonpublic places. I would like to see older couples holding hands, parents embracing and kissing each other with the kids around, couples exchanging a loving kiss during a picnic in the park. It would be rich to be able to say, "My husband and I had the most beautiful sex last night" as openly as we say "I ate the best food last night." The shroud we throw over the whole topic of sexuality has caused the topic to slide out as skewed gen-

der roles and a "street" version of sexuality learned through the informal network of peers and television. Many people carry damaging negative thoughts about sex and masturbation from their parents, who may have never acknowledged sex, or chastised their children for any indication of interest. Dr. Deborah Phillips has written an excellent book on unlearning these thoughts called *Sexual Confidence: Discovering the Joys of Intimacy.*

— A Touch of Health —

Touch is a biological need. Healers have used touch throughout human history, and the laying on of hands is still used today in spiritual and holistic health circles. The simple act of touching someone on the arm will lower blood pressure. Touch has provided breakthroughs in successfully reaching schizophrenic people; embracing them and giving rubdowns has opened emotional pathways that were previously blocked. Putting your arm around someone who is suffering an asthma attack will mitigate or halt the attack.

Animals instinctively lick, groom, cuddle, and touch each other. Even invertebrates are soothed by a gentle back-rubbing, and mammals seek a backscratch even in the absence of itching. Because we live in a no-touch culture, many people satisfy their daily need for cutaneous stimulation by fondling a pet. Petting an animal lowers a person's blood pressure, and pet ownership has been found to be the most influential variable in heart attack survival (even more than being married). My sister volunteers

for a successful pet therapy program through the Humane Society in which she and other volunteers bring puppies or kittens to nursing homes or children's hospital wards for patients to cuddle. The popularity of the program attests to its benefit.

Animals similarly benefit from being touched. In studies of rats with thyroids removed, 75 percent died in the control group, which received no petting or handling. In the other group, which received constant petting, only 13 percent died. The handled rats were more relaxed and accepting, while the unhandled rats were nervous, irritable, and tense. In a study at Ohio University, rabbits were fed a diet high in cholesterol. One group of rabbits was methodically touched, and one group not petted at all. The touched group had a 50 percent lower rate of arteriosclerosis than the untouched.

People derive definite medical benefits from touch. A friend worked one summer as head nurse of a nursing home. When she first arrived, there were people with bedsores the size of pie plates, despite the usual prescribed treatment of cleaning and medicating the sores, regularly turning the body, and putting sheepskin on the bed. Carol immediately began a touch program; the residents were massaged daily, and by the end of the summer virtually all the bedsores had disappeared. The massaging increased circulation, the extra bloodflow carrying nutrients to the sore areas, and the emotional satisfaction from pleasurable massage enabled healing.

Therapeutic touch, developed in the 1970s by Dolores Krieger, Ph.D., a professor at New York University, is now

taught at nursing schools around the country. More than 30,000 registered nurses practice it, as well as thousands of non-medical people. Therapeutic touch practitioners work with the "universal life energy," which they can feel by sweeping their hands a few inches above a person's body. To heal or ease pain, the practitioner identifies places where the evenness of the energy is broken, and "moves" energy there. Unhealthy energy can translate to the hands as heat, coolness, thickness, pressure, heaviness, or tingling, while healthy flow is comfortable in the hands and evenly distributed. Studies done by Krieger showed that therapeutic touch raised hemoglobin levels. This same friend who worked in the nursing home found it alarming that when she was caring for people she could tell before anyone else when they were going to die. She told me they "felt" different to her.

Skin grafting has been a common medical procedure, especially for burn victims. Transplanting skin from one person to another rarely works, as the donor skin is invariably rejected. Therefore, thin grafts of skin are taken from areas of the burn patient that were not damaged. Taking the graft itself creates another wound, so patients who are burned over the majority of their bodies cannot donate skin to themselves. This dilemma has been remedied by the advent of artificial skin, which is "grown" by placing skin cells in a soup of nutrients, vitamins, and collagen. Thin sheets of skin develop, and can be used for grafts. The cultured skin is also replacing some animal testing in the cosmetic industry. Without a blood supply it cannot redden or inflame in response to a toxic substance, but it does release the same chemical distress signals as damaged skin cells.

— What a Pain —

We want to avoid pain. Or do we? We drag sharp blades across our faces to remove hair, or pour hot wax on our legs and rip it off. We wear pointed, high-heeled shoes. We tattoo and circumcise. We pierce ears and noses. We even use painful events to initiate each other into certain clubs and fraternities. All these are choices humans make as part of our cultures, and all these cause pain.

Pain is largely beneficial. It demands action to eliminate what's causing it; you jerk a finger out of the flame, see a doctor, rest a sore knee. Your body's acute sense of pain, however uncomfortable, protects you from further damage. While receptors that sense heat and cold are fairly well developed at birth, a sense of pain doesn't develop until hours later (infants cry more out of shock than pain in response to a doctor's slap). This biological advantage makes sense; an acute sense of pain would be detrimental to an infant during birth.

Many cultures use pain to achieve certain purposes. Enduring great pain for a noble purpose has always been admired in religious and military realms. People are declared saints when martyred and awarded medals of honor for suffering war injuries. The Sioux practice the Sundance Ceremony in which people who have devoted themselves to the Great Spirit for four years fast, dance, and pierce their chests or arms with wooden sticks attached by strings to a large tree. They lean back against the tension until ultimately the skin breaks. The ceremony is a culmination of their sacrifice.

Many cultures circumcise boys as part of a rite of manhood, encouraging Spartan tolerance of the pain. Women may also go through painful initiation rites, which may include a circumcision that destroys or removes the clitoris.

Though we accept pain and even choose it in certain instances, generally we try to avoid it. Pain seems to be very subjective; expectations have much to do with how it is perceived. I find it more painful to be pricked in the finger to draw blood than to accidentally pierce my fingertip with a pin; trepidation magnifies the sensation at the Bloodmobile. (Fortunately for me, the Red Cross now offers the option of pricking the earlobe, which has very few pain receptors.) North American culture expects childbirth to be monumentally painful, while in some countries women simply stop their work in the fields, have their babies, and return to work afterward.

For several years, I experienced a six-week headache each fall. The first time it occurred, the pain was so intense and stretched on so endlessly, I felt life could not go on. The second and third time it occurred, I knew it would go away at its appointed time. Rather than threatening my continued enjoyment of life, the headache became much easier to bear with this frame of mind.

Pain is perceived when nerve endings lying just under the surface of the epidermis are stimulated, sending an electric impulse down the length of a neuron to the spinal cord, which sends it up to the brain to be interpreted. The sending of an impulse does not guarantee a pain sensation, however; the mind can override the signal and conquer the pain. Yogis marching over hot coals or athletes intent on the game short-circuit the pain

response through meditation or deep absorption in something. Biofeedback can be used to train the body not to feel pain, and is used to help chronic sufferers take control of their pain. Acupressure, reflexology, and acupuncture are often effective treatments for pain; they can stimulate the body to produce endorphins, natural opiates that occupy receptor sites so they can't receive the message of pain. Massage, which touches many acupressure and reflexology pressure points, is often used for relieving pain. My massage therapist treats headaches by having people lie on their backs. Then she presses her palms on the person's forehead with all her weight. The relief is extraordinary and lasts for hours.

We can deliver our own dose of endorphins simply by exercising. Even twenty minutes of exercise can release enough of these natural pain-stoppers to subdue pain. Distance runners and other athletes who exercise for long periods even experience a "high" that feels so good they seek it over and over. Endorphin levels also rise as a pregnant woman nears her delivery time. Women in general have higher pain thresholds than men, and experience pain routinely as part of the menstrual cycle. Many women understand the sensations not as negative pain but as an increased sense of power and vitality at this particularly psychic and wise time of their cycles.

Pain can also be inhibited simply by switching attention to something else. When my dentist delivers a needleful of Novocain, she uses the common technique of stretching and jiggling my cheek with her finger. I always thought it was to help the Novocain disperse. "No," she said, "it's just to distract you." She is banking on "lateral inhibition," where a bunch of neurons all try

to respond at once and get into a neural traffic jam. If you crack your elbow into a door, and rub the area around it, the pain will subside in the mass of sensation. The same principal applies to putting ice on bruises. It reduces swelling, and will also confuse the body by sending cold messages instead of pain messages. Capsaicin, which gives red chili peppers their reknowned hotness, is used in pain creams to be applied topically. It is considered to be a counter-irritant, confusing nerve cells so sensation in the skin substitutes for deeper pain. It may also upset the chemical balance inside sensory nerve cells that relay pain messages from the skin. During sex or sports, we easily ignore a certain amount of pain. It may be that the brain is receiving so many signals of pleasure that some pain messages get lost in the crowd.

Pain can be eased by anesthetic drugs like novocaine or cocaine that either block the body's ability to send pain signals to the brain or prevent sodium from flowing into a nerve cell. Aspirin blocks pain impulses by inhibiting the flow of substances that stimulate pain receptors. The beneficial effect of any analgesic can be reduced by continuous use, as found by sufferers of arthritis or back pain who may be long-term users of these drugs.

Not all pain originates at a free nerve ending; some is produced right up in the brain itself. Up to 70 percent of amputees sense pain in a "phantom limb," which may have been gone for many years. Even if not painful, perceived sensation in the nonexistent limb can be confusing; someone whose brain is telling him that the arm he doesn't have is sticking straight out to the side will find the message so real he'll turn sideways to walk through a doorway. A brain lesion in the parietal lobe, which controls body

image and recognition, can result in the opposite problem: "unilateral neglect," in which the sufferer denies ownership of a perfectly functional part of his body. He may shave only one side of his face, or shove away the "stranger's" leg inexplicably attached to his body.

— "Touchy" Communication —

If I don't like someone, she "rubs me the wrong way." An especially poignant film is "touching." That irritable person is "touchy," and you have to "get the feel" for how to "handle" him. Beauty is only "skin deep." You either "keep in touch" or "lose touch" with someone, and give "positive strokes" to encourage a person. People can be described as thick-skinned, thin-skinned, or as someone who gets under one's skin. We ask, "How do you feel it went?" and respond, "I think she handled it very tactfully." The word "tact" comes from the Latin *tactus*, from *tangere*, "to touch." Something very real to us is "tangible." A situation can be sticky, thorny, ticklish, or require kid gloves. When someone's mind is not what it used to be, we say they're a bit "touched." A crisis may be "touch and go," a holdover from horse-and-carriage days when the wheels of two carriages would glance off each other, but not snag.

Clearly our vibrant sense of touch has infused our language. Touch can help us communicate in other ways as well. In an experiment at Purdue University Library, a librarian touched someone unobtrusively half the time. The touched people later reported that she smiled at them (she didn't) but did not think

she'd touched them. In another test, waitresses lightly touched customers, and consistently garnered higher tips. If unobtrusive touch from a stranger can elicit a positive emotional response, think how much more powerful is the intentional, positive touch of a loved one.

The skin allows us further means of communication. In the embryo, skin develops from the same layers of cells as the eyes, and like the retina of the eye, has sensory receptors laid out in a pattern. This allows skin to pick up "images" and transmit them to the brain. For example, electronic devices can vibrate in an outline identical to letters of the alphabet, enabling a blind person to "see" when the skin is exposed to the vibrations. Another device allows a blind person to recognize geometric patterns, chairs, telephones, even faces, by feeling an array of electrodes sent to the skin by a camera the person wears. Abdominal skin "sees" better than the back or forearms. Touch also allows blind people to read at great speed using Braille. This must be developed; when I try to distinguish letters in Braille, I cannot tell how many dots are in each figure. Yet were I to train my fingertips, I could improve their sensitivity. One study showed how touch can compensate for deficiencies in other senses. Sixteen hooded students, in total darkness for one week, experienced a marked increase in skin sensitivity.

Skin can communicate in unconscious ways as well. It can be a window into the emotional state of an individual. Victims who remember physical and sexual abuse can wake up with "body memories": bruises, soreness, or other physical manifestations of the remembered events. Itching is often produced psychosomatically, and can be an unconscious striving for attention that was

denied in early life. People with chronic itching, called pruritis, almost always show disturbances in sexuality and hostility. The deprivation of love may cause eczema. Stress manifests itself in the skin; it stimulates the adrenal gland to produce steroids that cause increased oil production in the skin, causing pimples and blotches. Stress often releases the herpes viruses that the majority of us carry and people develop cold sores as a result.

— Unlearning the Silly Rules —

On a camping trip in the Chihuahan desert of Texas, my traveling partner suddenly snapped, "Stop touching everything!" I had been lightly dragging my fingers along rough rock that flanked a trail, feeling the softness of a cactus flower, testing one of the vicious points on a spiny bush, and sifting golden sand through my fingers. I was surprised and asked, "Why?" She had to think about it, and realized that it wasn't because she really wanted me to stop touching—in fact, she was yearning to touch as well—but that it was her mother's voice in her head as strong as thirty years prior: "Don't touch!"

We have a lot of unlearning to do. To truly enjoy our sense of touch we have to break social barriers that have been set up like police ribbon around a crime scene. If we want to look at something, we can do it surreptitiously or from afar; when we enjoy a smell on the air, no one has to know; if we listen to something, we don't have to let on. But to enjoy our tactile sense, we have to physically get in there and mix with things. The good news is that it is easy to do if a person decides that enjoying the gift of touch

is more important than abiding by some very silly rules that inhibit touch.

Silly Rule No. 1: Don't Get Dirty

Whoever coined "Cleanliness is next to Godliness" did humans a big disservice. Just for the record, Jesus was born in the hay of a stable (have you ever smelled a stable?), spat in the dirt to make a poultice for curing blindness, drew in the sand while thinking, and rode a burro. Cleanliness for the sake of health is certainly a good thing, but we have perverted the idea of general cleanliness to mean "Don't ever get dirty." Some of the most exhilarating times of my life have been when I was getting filthy: scrambling up a very dusty volcano; being buried (except for my head) in the sand; sweating like a racehorse during a cross country ski marathon; and slinging mud during a ten-person mudfight at a picnic which culminated in everyone jumping into the mudpit and wallowing.

Children are the best models for uninhibited enjoyment of the senses, especially touch. They will unabashedly reach for something, roll in something, and touch all parts of their bodies to things. When a baby enjoys a book, it is enjoyed in the mouth (a very sensitive touch organ), on the head, under the seat, and on the legs. Food is enjoyed the same way, and in all the same places. Getting dirty does not mitigate a child's desire to experience something—it often enhances it! We particularly do girls a disservice by parading them in delicate frills. When they start to

play, they are told to stop because it will wreck their clothes. Boys, however, are usually free to play in their more rough-and-tumble outfits.

Every time this staunch rule stops you from enjoying something, ask "Why not get dirty?" Certainly if you are on your way to a job interview and have a burning desire to splash in that rain puddle, you are smart to abide by the rule. But many times you are able to get clean again, and the mess is worth the enjoyment.

Silly Rule No. 2: Always Wear Clothes

Most of the time it's clothes that cause us to abide by the first rule. We have nice things, and don't want to wreck them. I am a firm believer in caring well for things you have. So, the best solution is to not wear clothes when you don't have to. Or, if you don't have the privacy you require, wear minimal clothes. Or clothes you specifically wear to get dirty.

Wearing clothes from birth onward desensitizes our sense of touch. Even during breastfeeding, one of life's most intimate touches, mother and baby are usually clothed. To regain full tactile sensitivity, you need to go naked once in awhile. Anyone who has skinnydipped can swear by the incredible feeling of unbroken sensation. A breeze coming through a window and caressing your whole skin is unlike any breeze you've felt before. Benjamin Franklin, Victor Hugo, and others believed they did their best writing in the nude. Notice how children pull off socks and shoes, even as babies. See how they protest getting dressed. They innately want to be unencumbered in experiencing the world.

At the Oregon Country Fair in Eugene, Oregon, I had my first exposure to tasteful public nudity. Being a reserved Mid-westerner, it had never occurred to me that going naked, outside, was an option. People left clothes in a cubbyhole at the gate of a large cedar fence, and entered an open air compound that included solar showers, a large fire for drying off, and a round, enclosed sixty-five-person cedar sauna. Men, women, and children were all enjoying heat, water, and wind on their whole skin, as normally as if they were at a school picnic. Once I realized that nobody cared what I looked like, and that unclothed people all look substantially alike, I could enjoy the beautiful sensations and ease of walking around as my natural self.

Find a place in your home where it feels good to be naked. It may be on a couch where sun shines in the afternoon, or in a breezy kitchen, or on a lambskin rug in your living room. Make a point to experience your whole skin regularly.

Silly Rule No. 3: Act Normal

First of all, nobody really cares what you do. Someone can be lying on the grass, rubbing bare feet on it, and passersby barely even glance. The way you will look when you stretch your usual boundaries will be much more normal than you feel. With practice, you'll get accustomed to doing what used to feel unusual, and you'll find that the range of normality stretches farther than you think. In a survey of old people, when asked what they would do differently in life, the most common answer was "Take more risks."

Silly Rule No. 4: Avoid Bodily Pleasures

Body pleasures are bad, hedonistic, nasty, primitive—you fill in the blank. Somewhere along the line, with the Puritans if not before, enjoying the senses got a bad name. Being holy was equated with denying oneself bodily pleasure. Relishing the sense of touch was especially bad, presumably because it could be related to sex. Freeing yourself from this fallacy will require a revision of your beliefs based on the gut reasons you picked up this book; that sensual living is a normal state of humanity and is necessary to live fully. I'm happy to report that once my camping friend realized the source of her irritation at my touching things, she could consciously fight it. By the end of the trip, she was urging me to take off my hiking boots and explore the Rio Grande barefoot.

Silly Rule No. 5: Always Be Productive

Real life takes time. When you look back, what are you going to wish you had done? Probably "I wish I had enjoyed myself more" and not "I wish I'd spent more time working."

— Let's Touch! —

As a child, I had heard of the legendary responsiveness of the blind to touch, and requested my mother to blindfold me for a day so I could experience such improvement in perception. She had to

explain that it takes longer than a day. Research on animals indicates that the parts of the brain involved in tactile perception can be expanded with the experience of touching. Tuning in tactually more often may actually change the brain to allow greater touch sensitivity. You don't have to be blindfolded; just consciously attuned. The experiences that follow will get you started.

Feeling Life

Read this activity, then put down the book and experience it for at least two minutes. Close your eyes, and wherever you are, tune into the tactile sensation of just being alive. Feel the heat inside your body. Notice the quiet, full feeling of life throughout your being. Savor the air rushing through your nose, pushing out your abdomen, filling your lungs and flowing back out. Sense where your limbs are positioned, what your shape is. If you have pain, acknowledge it. If you do not, appreciate the smooth, neutral feeling of no pain. Do your clothes feel rough? Smooth? Wiggle your toes; caress your teeth with your tongue. Think how you would describe to someone what it feels like to be alive. Now, put down the book and tune in to your existence.

Tactile Treats

This is a collection of some of my favorite touch sensations, internal and external. Write your own on slips of paper and keep them in a jar, to pull one out when you want to treat yourself (this is a

great substitute for caloric treats if you are watching your weight).

- Sleep naked on sun-dried sheets
- Get a professional massage
- Stretch
- Put on clothes straight out of the dryer
- Give yourself a foot rub
- Have someone wash your hair
- Feel fruits and vegetables: round citrus, fuzzy peach, bumpy squash
- Tickle palm with fingertips
- Lie down with a pleasantly full stomach
- Soak feet in hot water

Body Trip

Take off your clothes and relax somewhere private for this one. Close your eyes and clear your mind of distractions and your body of tensions. When you are ready, run your hands slowly down your body, feeling all its different textures—soft or bristly head hair, firm folded ears, paper-thin eyelids, pliant lips, hard jawbone, scoop under chin to neck, rise of chest, roundness of tummy, tangle of pubic hair, large muscles in thigh, irregularly shaped kneecap, flexible calf (push up and down on it as it hangs relaxed), bony ankles, intricate shape of heel, arch, and toes. Notice how the touch feels both to your hand and to the part of

you being explored. As you go, appreciate all that is good about your body; it houses all the senses and abilities you need to richly experience the world.

Ten-Minute Cat

Cats are experts at seeking pleasure in every moment. They always find the most comfortable spot in a room. They stretch luxuriously, and often. They arch their backs up to your hand or rub their bodies around your leg when they want petting. Spend ten minutes like a cat, denying yourself no impulse of pleasure-seeking. If you want to scratch your back against the door, roll on the grass, stretch to the sky, lounge in a sunny square on the floor — just do it. You may even want to nap (cats spend twenty hours a day sleeping) and feel the flood of total relaxation in your body.

Everyday Sensations

Mark Twain observed that the most overrated pleasure is intercourse and the most underrated is defecation. There are many daily things that we have been trained not to relish. Laundry is considered a chore, yet pulling hot fabrics out of the dryer and folding them is a very pleasurable tactile experience. Take a moment to feel the heated fabrics on your face. While mowing a lawn you can enjoy the vibration of the mower handle, the swing of your weight from one foot to the other as you walk along, the sun and breeze on your face. My favorite part of drinking tea is cupping my two hands around the mug and soaking in the heat.

Tune in to the lush tactile sensations each time you do these normally prosaic things:

- Use the toilet
- Walk up stairs
- Shower
- Yawn
- Get dressed
- Use a towel
- Undress
- Brush snow off the car
- Shake hands
- Knead dough
- Brush or comb hair
- Coil a rope, string, or yarn
- Put on lotion or oil
- Scour or sand something
- Write with a pen
- Stretch a rubber band
- Slide into cool sheets
- Whistle
- Wash and cut up vegetables

Water Wonders

I occasionally swim in the morning for variety in my fitness routine. Swimming is an extremely sensual sport, but I was rarely conscious of that, bent as I was on perfecting my stroke, counting laps, and working hard. Now I spend a few moments at the beginning and end of the swim to relish the feeling of water. At the beginning, the bracing water on warm skin sends a shock wave, which instantly changes to a silky flow as I start moving through the water. The reach and stretch of arms and the gentle swivel of shoulders and head seem stiff at first, but glide into an effortless motion once muscles and joints heat up. After the swim I treat myself to floating on my back, feeling the cushiony support of water, the beating of my heart, and the relaxed, drained feeling of exercised muscles.

Whether or not you swim, explore water for a sensual treat. You can do it in water that is only waist-deep.

- Slap the water. It's hard and will sting your hand. Now pet it. It's soft and will gently swallow your hand.
- Float on your back and enjoy the mysterious feeling of buoyancy. Sense the water against your hands as you move to stay afloat (although I know someone so buoyant she can cross her arms over her chest and literally fall asleep on top of the water).

- Lean back your head and move it slowly from side to side to swirl your hair in the water (this is especially wonderful with longer hair). The high concentration of touch receptors on the head makes the gentle back-and-forth pull of hair a massage from the inside out.
- Go nude in water (bath and shower don't count). Float, swim, or dogpaddle, but get your body completely naked and completely suspended in water. To have no part of your body touching a garment or a firm surface is to enter a heavenly new world of sensation.

Massage the Extremities

This involves a partner. I especially encourage spouses to do this as a way to be sensual together, and for parents to do this with their children to increase interaction and touch between generations.

Lie down on a comfortable but firm surface, like a carpeted floor. Your feet should be bare. Have your partner kneel at your feet and massage one foot, using firm touch so as not to tickle. The massager should touch every part of the foot—between toes, tips of toes, entire bottom and top of foot, heel, and area below the ankle. After two minutes, the massager should stop. Feel the difference between your two feet; it will be as if they belong to different people. The massaged foot will be alive and vibrant,

while the other foot will feel dull in comparison. Now have the other foot massaged the same way. Switch places.

You can vary this exercise by massaging the hands, scalp, face, or back of your partner.

A New Look at Pain

The next time you have pain, be it a headache, premenstrual cramps, or a throbbing stubbed toe, try viewing it as a normal and tolerable part of life. I always marveled at our family dog, who could have her tail shut in a door and yet maintain her sunny disposition. I knew it probably hurt for hours, but she went on with life as usual.

Try your body's powerful natural means of relief before popping pills:

- Exercise to release endorphins and reduce the stress that causes the vast majority of headaches.
- Do deep relaxation of your entire body.
- Get a massage.
- Press acupressure points associated with the painful area (there are many good books on this). For example, headaches are relieved by firmly squeezing the place where the bones of your forefinger and thumb meet. Use the forefinger and thumb of the other hand to press the spot from both above and below. Menstrual pain is relieved when someone presses two spots above and on either side of your tailbone.

- Distract yourself from the pain by deluging the area with other sensations. For example, rub your lower abdomen when you have menstrual cramps, or massage the finger you just hit with a hammer.
- Don't forget to see what's good about it. Did that "funny bone" make you more alert? Is the stomachache really telling you to slow down and enjoy your life in a more relaxed way?

Look Ma, No Hands

With nerves highly concentrated in the fingers and palms, humans naturally use hands to touch most things. However, to gain a new tactile view, use other sensitive parts of your body to feel things. Your face, lips, and genitals are packed with tactile receptors. Feel a feather on any of these spots, and it is a different feather from the one your hands touch. A soft or silky cloth is exquisite. I love to pet a cat with my face, feeling the caress of fur on my cheeks and lips, and the flick of tail brushing my eyelids. Open your mind to touching things with more than your hands.

Try it right now: how does the cover of this book feel against your face? Try turning the page with just your sensitive lower lip. Now feel the pleasure of pressing your lips firmly on the page.

Temperature Trick

This experience shows that our sense of touch is relative. Put one hand in a bowl of hot water, the other in a bowl of cold. After

twenty to thirty seconds, submerge both hands in tepid water. You will feel the tepid water as two different temperatures.

This same principle works on a larger scale; when spring days bring sixty-degree weather after a long cold winter, Minnesotans cavort outside in T-shirts and shorts. However, after a hot summer, a sixty-degree autumn day sends the same people running for sweaters and jeans.

Slumber Party Specialty (Back-writing)

Pull up your shirt to reveal your bare back. Have a partner draw a letter of the alphabet on your skin with a finger, and you guess what it is from the sensation. When this gets too easy, progress to whole words.

Sensual Holiday

For people who have been together a long time, sex can take on a certain routine. To revive the sensuality in your relationship, get out of your usual location and schedule, be it for a week or a weekend. Take turns planning it, as a surprise for the other. The whole purpose should be to simply enjoy each other and the sensations you give each other. The first day, abstain from intercourse, and use the time instead to revive pleasing and touching each other in other ways. Just as each individual sense gets desensitized to repeated stimuli, so does a relationship. The change of place and pace will enliven all the senses and refocus attention on each other.

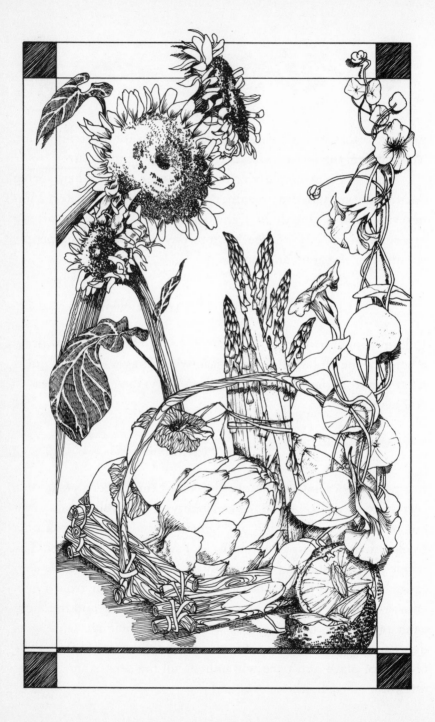

3

Taste:
The Cultural Sense

Caucasians crave tall, thick milkshakes; Chinese gag at the thought of drinking mammary secretions. Southeast Asians consider giant waterbugs a delicacy; Europeans and Americans abhor the thought of eating insects. A Californian would never consider eating a garden slug, but pays a premium for escargot, snails of the same species. The French commonly eat horsemeat, while Americans consider it dog food.

Even our definitions of what constitutes a meal vary from culture to culture. In parts of Africa, one must have porridge to make a meal; Europeans require bread; Asians, rice; Mexicans, beans; North Americans, meat or fish.

Despite differences in food preferences, every culture uses food for more than just nourishment.

Food forges and maintains human relationships. It represents wealth or status, such as when someone serves caviar at a dinner party, or celebrates a heroic act by sharing a feast with the village. Food often forms the outward sign of spiritual rites, such as bread and wine at Christian communion, unleavened bread and bitter herbs for Jewish passover, harvest offerings in Native American ceremonies, and cow's milk for bathing statues in Hindu temples. Food helps celebrate the biggest events in life: births, deaths, and weddings. Food and drink seal business deals, and cement reunions of family and kin. Eating and drinking give us a common meeting point; they are some of the few activities in which all humans participate, every day. It is no wonder that the local pub becomes a common social focal point, or that we go out for dinner with someone special.

— In the Tongue Groove —

About three months after conception, taste buds begin forming in a fetus. They are located in tiny protrusions covering the fetus's tongue, roof of mouth, tonsils, and down the throat. Adults have 10,000 taste buds, concentrated mainly on the tongue. Cattle have 25,000 taste buds, the bloodhound equivalent in the taste arena. Inside each of our buds is about fifty cells that relay taste sensations to the brain. Taste buds specializing in the four main tastes are clustered together like teams before a scrimmage: the tip of the tongue holds cells most sensitive to sweet flavors; the sides sport leaflike protrusions that sense sour; mushroom-like protrusions scattered across the surface perceive salt; and pitlike structures near the back taste bitter.

Infants have an inborn preference for sweet tastes, and have the ability to taste sour, bitter, and salty. Evolutionists speculate that humans evolved a sweet tooth because sweet foods usually indicated a good source of carbohydrates, or energy, and thus were advantageous for survival in a natural environment where energy-laden foods were not freely available. Likewise, our natural affinity for salt was an essential adaptation to guarantee we ingested enough salt to maintain cellular functions. Our sensitivity to bitter tastes, and the gag reflex that often accompanies it, kept us from ingesting toxic substances. We can detect sweetness in as low a concentration as one part in 200; our threshold for salt is even more sensitive, at one part in 400; sourness is detected at just one part in 130,000; and bitter, with the lowest threshold, can be detected at one part in 2,000,000. This works to our biological advantage, as most poisons are bitter.

Today, many humans have sweet and salty foods readily available, and our natural affinity for them causes us to eat far more than we need. Half of all sugar used in America sweetens soda pop, which has no nutritional value. Even cereal, a mainstay of breakfast, often wears a sweet coating; some cereals have as much sugar by weight as a candy bar. Similarly, with salt being inexpensive and widely available, we ingest many times what is needed by the body, which results in high blood pressure, one of the major health problems in developed countries.

Some differences in taste perception are purely cultural, such as the recent acceptance of Japanese-style raw fish by Americans, who have long been amenable to eating raw clams and oysters. However, some tastes actually are different for different people, as there are some variations in the tasting mechanism. Heredity

equips some of us with sensitivity to a substance in artichokes (and to a lesser extent asparagus) that causes water to taste sweet when drunk after eating these foods. Heredity also determines which two-thirds of us can taste the bitter phenylthiocarbamide, or PTC; those who have this taste sense find caffeine and saccharin bitter. This may explain why some people find diet soft drinks unpleasant. Variations in the ability to taste salt reflects the amount of salt in each person's saliva, a level which fluctuates according to such things as body chemistry and amount of exercise. The more sodium present, the more accustomed a person is to it, and the more sodium he or she requires to give food a salty taste. People who need little salt may have such low levels of sodium in their saliva that they can taste the naturally-occurring sodium in foods.

Taste sensation can also be altered by eating substances that enhance or inhibit another taste. Take for example the famed toothpaste-and-orange juice effect, in which orange juice tastes unpleasant after brushing the teeth. Toothpaste contains detergents to break down the structure of fat in food particles so they can be washed away. Taste bud membrane is composed of a fat-based phospholipid. Therefore, toothpaste temporarily breaks down the membrane, leaving it raw and interfering with the taste of sugar in the juice. Other chemicals in toothpaste then exaggerate the sourness of the ascorbic and citric acids in the juice.

West African natives chew on a berry they call the "miracle fruit," because it causes sour substances to taste sweet. Imagine being able to eat a lemon as if it were a candy! Salt enhances sweetness (many people put salt on cantaloupe and honeydew melon for this very reason), whereas acid suppresses sweetness.

Taste accounts for a very small part of overall flavor. Smell plays a much bigger role, giving us the infinite variations of flavor that the four tastes of sweet, salty, sour, and bitter cannot detect. Cane sugar, maple sugar, and honey all have the same sweet taste; only the aroma varies. Smell is more sensitive than taste; it takes twenty-five times more molecules of apple crisp to taste than to smell. Texture and temperature also contribute to flavor.

As people age, the number of taste buds declines. By age seventy-five, people lose two-thirds of the taste buds they had at age thirty. Sensitivity to sweet diminishes from youth, which makes sense biologically; when young, a child needs large amounts of energy to grow, while older people have less need for highly caloric foods. Sensitivity to salt also fades, requiring more salt to be added to food to perceive the same taste as during youth. Children under age six have the most taste sensitivity, which may explain why children are often finicky eaters.

— Good to Eat or Good to Think? Food Taboos —

Like bears, pigs, rats, and cockroaches, humans are omnivores, meaning we eat a wide variety of both plant and animal foods. We have seemingly limitless possibilities of edibles, compared to creatures like the koala bear, which exists entirely on the leaves of a certain species of eucalyptus tree. Like rodents, our mouths sport cutting incisors; like horses and other herbivores, grinding molars and premolars; like tigers and other carnivores, pointed canines.

We have been hunter-gatherers for more than 99 percent of our several million year history, so our adaptation to eating a wide variety of food was important to survival in unpredictable conditions. When hunting was poor, we could subsist on plant foods; when drought devastated fruit trees and tubers, we could prey on other animals. Mostly we combined the two as best we could, much as modern primates purposely choose fruits with the worm.

Yet with earth offering perhaps 20,000 edible plants, why do we only cultivate about 600? And why does every culture have taboos on certain foods which are considered edible in other societies? Claude Levi-Straus of the College de France proposed that human attitudes toward what is and is not food have less to do with what is good to eat than with what is "good to think" in that particular society. There will always be conventions regarding which foods are edible, or suitable for certain occasions. Anthropologists have found that food "riddles" which seem irrational and perplexing at first are actually appropriate adaptations to a set of conditions. Take, for example, the classic "irrational" food taboo: India's sacred cow. Here is a highly populated country, teetering on malnutrition, where it is forbidden to eat a cow. Cows are venerated, bedecked with blossoms, cared for by the government when sick, and allowed to wander freely. The population struggles for enough animal protein. And yet, no one disputes the sacredness of the cow.

It hardly seems that this can be rational until one knows more about the situation. In his book, *The Sacred Cow and the Abominable Pig*, Marvin Harris explains the many circumstances leading to the prohibition on eating cows. Briefly, they are:

1. Oxen (castrated cattle) are essential to the Indian agricultural system. Crops are grown on privately owned ten-acre plots. Oxen provide the power necessary to till the soil. Since everyone's harvest ripens at the same time, sharing of oxen is not possible. Therefore, each farmer must own oxen. Cows are necessary to get oxen.

2. During drought, cows are infertile, but it still does not make sense to eat them. Once conditions improve, the hardy breed becomes fertile again. The cow stores nutrients and water in its shoulder hump, much like a camel, thereby relieving the family from sharing scarce resources with it. It is advantageous for government to house barren or sick cows when a family cannot, as the value of a live cow is so much greater than when it is dead.

3. Owners allow the cows to wander so that the cows do not have to be fed. The cows, adapted to the harsh environment, forage on roadside grasses. Thus the cow imposes no strain on an impoverished family's resources.

4. Due to the heavy demands of overpopulation, wood is scarce in India. Yet everyone needs fuel daily for heat and cooking. Cow dung serves this purpose, effectively recycling unusable grasses and weeds into essential fuel. The dung also provides vital natural fertilizer for the fields. In some places in India, farmers recycle fully 100 percent of dung for these purposes. Again, the cow is more valuable alive than eaten.

5. The breed of cow that survives well in India differs from the fat feedlot heifer in America. Not a generous meat source, it does continually provide the owners with animal protein in the form of milk, which is used to make yogurt. When a cow finally

dies naturally, the lowest social caste, known as the Untouch-
ables, eats the meat and makes leather from the hide, providing a
kind of welfare system for India's poorest.

Any one of these reasons alone points to the sense in not eating cows in India. Combined, it is clear that to eat the cows would
spell disaster. America's "sacred cow," the dog, makes much less
sense since it performs no useful work, is not used as a food
source, and competes with humans for animal protein. Imagine
other cultures' disbelief in our having special doctors, schools, and
cemeteries for our dogs. Think how disgusting it could appear
that dogs roam freely in our houses. How ridiculous that we experience grief akin to a relative dying when the dog passes away.
How incomprehensible that we don't even make use of the meat
or hide once a dog dies (some Asian cultures routinely eat nutritious dog meat).

People of northern European descent consider milk and
dairy products an essential part of a normal, healthy diet. They
are one of the few groups on earth who drink milk as adults; they
are far outnumbered by the rest of the world's people, who actually get ill from milk and consider it abnormal to drink it as an
adult. In fact, the adult human is not naturally suited to drinking
milk. Most people in the world lack sufficient amounts of lactase,
the enzyme that breaks down the lactose (sugar) in milk. While
human infants have sufficient lactase to digest their mother's milk,
this tolerance disappears in early childhood. From a survival
standpoint, both in humans and other mammals, this was essential: loss of lactase prevents adults from competing with infants
for milk. An adult who drank milk would experience cramps,
diarrhea, severe intestinal gas, and sometimes vomiting.

Then why do people of northern European descent drink milk, and experience a 90 percent lactose tolerance in their population? Like other "strange" food habits, this is an adaptation that aided survival. Groups that lived far from the equator were highly susceptible to rickets, a bone disease caused by a lack of Vitamin D, which is necessary for absorption of calcium by the body. People living in sunny climes had no problem; an abundance of sunshine allowed their skin to produce all the Vitamin D they needed, so calcium from foods like dark leafy vegetables was fully utilized. About 10,000 years ago, people domesticated milk-producing animals. Those in northern climates who were lactose-tolerant had a higher survival (and thus reproduction) rate because they could digest milk, which provided abundant calcium. This selective advantage eventually produced a genetic tolerance for milk in these northern groups. Milk drinkers are descended from people who tended to keep cattle, drink milk, and live far from the equator. A few African tribes also drink milk, and show an 80 percent lactose tolerance in their population. Some other cultures consume yogurt and cheese, which possess relatively small amounts of lactose due to the fermentation by bacteria. The Inuit and other people in arctic climates get calcium from eating the bones and marrow of their kill.

Americans and Europeans abominate insects, which in most cultures is not the case. All around the world, people are especially fond of locusts, grasshoppers, crickets, ants, termites, and the larvae and pupae of large moths, butterflies, and beetles (they don't have the hard shell, or chitin, of the adult versions). Insect flesh is almost as nourishing as meat or poultry; a mere handful of locusts provides an adult with all the protein, Vitamin A, and fat

required in a day. Before the arrival of Europeans, native people in what is now California depended heavily on insects for sustenance. Locusts and the young, fat larvae of bees, wasps, ants, and moths provided food all year long, either fresh or dried for the winter months. Laotians, Vietnamese, and Thais enjoy giant water bugs; inhabitants of Madagasgar, the Kalahari, the West Indies, and New Caledonia eat spiders (not technically an insect, but similar for the purpose of example). Before the invention of soap and insecticides, lice were a plague for humans as they are for other primates, and family members would pick them off each other and pop them into their mouths.

I attended a seminar on edible insects at a local county park to help balance my narrow American upbringing that says insects aren't good to eat. I wasn't exactly new to insectivory, having swallowed many a gnat and mosquito while mountain biking, or inadvertently eaten an ant on my food at a picnic. However, to intentionally seek out bugs for food was a new idea. We flushed grasshoppers from a field, caught them in butterfly nets, and brought them back inside to fry them up into crispy treats. With a dash of salt, they tasted much like a corn chip, and were very pleasurable. Samplings of "John the Baptist Bread" (made with locusts and honey), and "Chocolate Chirp Cookies" (containing crickets) proved that insects could be a nutritional addition to many foods. I still cannot bring myself to eat fly maggots, however, despite the fact that the Chinese, until recently, regularly feasted on them. My culturization is too strong.

The reasons for eating or refusing to eat insects are outgrowths of the "optimal foraging" theory: an organism will seek the food that gives the most value for the amount of work

expended to obtain it. This principle applies to all creatures, including humans. Dr. Lynn Rogers, internationally reknowned bear researcher in Ely, Minnesota, has found that black bears will kill and eat a deer fawn if they happen upon it conveniently, yet do not hunt for fawns as a regular part of their diet. It doesn't pay to expend energy hunting for fawns when other foods, like fat caterpillars, are available in large quantity for little effort.

This theory applies to humans as well. While killing a wildebeest may provide an African tribe with a large amount of protein, the scarcity and difficulty of obtaining a wildebeest may not be worth the trouble when termite larvae are readily available in nests as big as houses, and dried termites are 45 percent protein (higher than dried fish). Cultures that do not have large vertebrates, like domesticated animals, readily available will be likely to practice insectivory. Cultures that have large vertebrates available will not find it worth the caloric cost of obtaining small and possibly scattered insects. These logical choices become a culturized food pattern, and thus, an American cannot imagine eating fried maggots while someone in New Guinea serves them as a delicacy.

Cannibalism is another adaptive food preference or taboo. While most people can forgive cannibalism under duress, such as the California Donner Pass survivors in 1847, or the Uruguayan rugby team whose plane crashed in the Andes in 1972, most cultures eschew anthropophagy. Again, the attitude can be traced to the conditions experienced by different groups. It is not as simple as "primitive" versus "sophisticated"; the Aztecs, one of the world's most advanced and sophisticated cultures, practiced cannibalism on the largest scale ever known.

Anthropologists have found that need for food is not typically a reason for people to kill each other, but rather an adaptation to using human flesh that has already been obtained through natural death or the culture's usual practices of war and religious sacrifices. Some New Guinea tribes have the custom of eating relatives who have died naturally; these tribes also have little access to protein foods in their environment. The Aztecs were a large population, and similarly had no large vertebrates to hunt or domesticate. Frogs and insects were available but were not practical for feeding millions of people. Human sacrifices were part of elaborate religious rituals, and provided protein as well.

The main reason some cultures prohibit cannibalism is not that they have a higher moral standard: cannibalism became taboo when it was economically advantageous for the culture to *not* eat people. A community that is organized as a small village, for example, may be living at subsistence level. A prisoner of war from another village provides much more value as a meal than as another mouth to feed. However, in places where the political organization is a state or kingdom, where subjects engage in activities like agriculture or crafts that could produce a surplus, it is more advantageous to put a prisoner of war to work at producing this surplus than it is to eat him, especially since domesticated animals are probably available. Cannibalism was practiced in Europe until the political organization changed to a state where it was more beneficial for the society as a whole not to cannibalize. Again, the cultural adaptation eventually became woven into the fabric of society.

In their book, *Consuming Passions: The Anthropology of Eating*, Peter Farb and George Armelagos describe many odd food habits

that were adaptations beneficial for survival. For example, the British habit of adding milk to tea neutralizes the tannin in tea, a substance linked to cancer. Clearly, in a culture where tea is a central beverage, those who preferred milk with tea would have a better chance of survival. Central and South Americans who add limestone to the soaking water of their maize are getting calcium that is otherwise unavailable in their diet. Pregnant women in west Africa eat nutrient-rich clay from termite mounds. The clay compares favorably with mineral supplements prescribed in the United States. Ethiopian "chow" contains up to fifteen spices, the combination of which has been shown to inhibit the effect of microorganisms like staphylococcus and salmonella. About one quarter of the people in the world eat chili pepper, and most of these people live in hot climates. The capsaicin in chili pepper causes a person to sweat, effectively lowering body temperature. Chili pepper is one of the most widely used spices in the world, surpassing almost all other plants as a source of Vitamin A, and providing Vitamins B and C.

Differing food aversions and preferences among people within the same culture do occur. People and animals prefer food that is familiar, so someone exposed to many kinds of food will have a wider field of preferences than someone raised on a narrow diet. I offered a fresh peach to a man who grew up twelve miles from where I did; as I bit with relish into my peach, he winced and looked around for a knife to peel his before eating it. He had been taught that the skin was not to be eaten, while I was taught to eat the skin of almost everything.

Aversions to food can be acquired by experiencing illness after eating a food, even if a person knows that the food did not

cause the illness. I steer clear of okra, because I vomited shortly after having okra for the first time. It turned out I had the flu, but I still cannot separate the experience from okra.

This principle has spawned experiments to discover pest control methods. It has been found that coyotes who prey on sheep from western ranches develop an aversion to sheep after eating a carcass laced with lithium chloride, which makes the coyote ill. Appalachian women in the early twentieth century kept rats from eating their wallpaper by mixing wallpaper paste with chili pepper, a substance to which rats have an aversion.

Food preferences may occur through the body's natural yearning for something it needs. Pregnant women often have desires for unusual foods, many of which aid production of serotonin, which aids the body in alleviating pain. The cravings are often for ice cream and other dairy products, and for sweet things like chocolate and fruit, because the body has a high need for calcium and extra calories during pregnancy. In places such as China, where people do not consume milk and milk products, a pregnant woman craves sweet-and-sour spareribs. Vinegar in the recipe draws out calcium from the rib bones into the meat, making it available to the body. This is called "specific hunger," and is thought to spur people with high nutritional demands to seek what they need. It can result in pica, which is the repeated eating of a nonnutritive substance for at least one month.

In the southern United States, there are clay banks with hundreds of spoon holes in them, and people share knowledge of the best clay spots. Pregnant women often crave certain minerals that are present in clay, and earth-eating is widely practiced around the world. Probably introduced to America by Africans,

clay-eating has become a habit for many. It is eaten "raw," or baked to a dry cracker, and may provide iron, a mineral in high demand for a pregnant woman. Some habitual clay eaters, upon moving to northern United States urban areas where clay is not available, take to eating dry laundry starch, which has the same texture as clay. This can result in health disturbances, as can another form of pica, children's eating of paint (perhaps for the sweet taste of lead).

— Kiss Me or Pass the Oysters —

Almost any food qualifies as an aphrodisiac, a food that supposedly increases sexual potency, because the act of eating produces the same physical changes associated with orgasm: sweating, raised body temperature, and increased pulse rate and blood pressure. Certain foods were probably endowed with the label of aphrodisiac because of their resemblance to genitals: the sea slug enlarges when touched; oysters and clams look like female genitalia; eels and snakes are phallic. Vegetables and fruits were also popular for the same reasons; bananas, cherries, dates, figs, peaches, celery, cucumbers, garlic, and leeks have all been considered boons to sexuality. The Elizabethans regarded prunes as so intense an aphrodisiac that they were served free in brothels.

Parts of animals related to reproduction were often thought to be aphrodisiacs, such as fish roe, swan genitals, various bird eggs, and the musk glands of deer. Other foods took on reproductive connotations because the species of animal was known

for fecundity. Thus, various parts of goats and rabbits have been popularized.

The mouth is as powerful a sex organ as the genitals. The tongue and lips are even endowed with the same nerve structures called "Krause's end bulbs" that are found in the clitoris and tip of penis. Food has been linked to sex in our language, as when we describe an attractive woman as "a tart," "a dish," "a hot tomato," "a honey pot," or "good enough to eat." The Bible's Song of Songs freely associates food with attraction: "To me your breasts are like bunches of grapes, your breath like the fragrance of apples, and your mouth like the finest wine." A lover's cheeks are "as lovely as a garden that is full of herbs and spices." Love is "better than wine." A verse also reads, "The taste of honey is on your lips, my darling; your tongue is milk and honey for me." Like Solomon, we too associate our lovers with food, using nicknames like "sweetie," "sweetheart," "sugar," "honey," and "sweetie pie."

— Food Talk —

Our language uses food terms for more than just sexual references. A complaint is a "beef," and someone can be full of "baloney." My father tells "corny jokes," and "hams it up"; he "peppers" his speech with humor. When I wanted to drive his "lemon," I "buttered him up." Our family often sits around and "chews the fat." A friend may ask what's "eating" you; perhaps you are "waffling" on a decision.

A feeling can be "delicious." Something "smacks" of foul play. "Pork-barrel projects" corrupt our government. A poorly made item is "cheesy." That body-builder is a "beefcake," and may

be a real "meat-and-potatoes man." Children say "pretty please with sugar on top" to entice permission. You got a "sweet" deal on that car, but the salesperson left "a bad taste in your mouth." People can have a "sour" personality, or be "bitter" over something. You might describe a rugged character as "salty"; an active and interesting person as "spicy"; a genius as an "egghead." Success is so close you can "taste" it.

Words can cause us to salivate, as when I tell you I just bit into a peeled lime. My salivary glands immediately prepare for sweetness upon the mention of a pastry. A substance must be dissolved for us to taste it, so our mouths are bathed in saliva. When food enters the mouth, enzymes in saliva begin the digestive process immediately. The taste nerves immediately signal nearby salivary glands to produce.

— Barriers to Good Taste —

To keep your sense of taste in tip-top shape, there are three things to avoid. Each of these inhibits your enjoyment of the myriad of flavors available every day.

Smoking

As noted in Chapter One, smoking has been shown to significantly deaden one's sense of smell, which is a major component in the ability to taste. Smoking also leaves a strong, bitter taste on the tongue and in saliva that interferes with other flavors by either changing or obscuring them.

Excess Salt, Sugar, and Fat

Affinity for these three tastes is biologically programmed into us, as these elements were difficult to obtain in the wild and were essential to survival. The challenge for humans in developed countries where these things are available in abundance is to limit our consumption. Health reasons that support limiting these foods are widely known. However, the effect on taste is usually overlooked. Studies have shown that people who reduce their consumption of salt gradually come to prefer less salt; the same has been shown with sugar. These tastes are so strong they obscure the more subtle natural tastes in food. By gradually reducing your use of salt and sugar, you will begin tasting and appreciating many new things. A friend often eats raw carrots as a treat. He consumes so little refined sugar that the sweetness of carrots is like candy to him. I never add sugar to cold cereal or oatmeal anymore; the natural sugars in grains are delicious alone. Eat melon without salt, and grapefruit without sugar. Fat has the same obscuring effect over other flavors as salt and sugar. Try to not butter vegetables and simply savor their fresh, pungent flavors for what they are.

Extremes of Hot and Cold

Americans drink their beer ice cold, while the more connoisseuring Europeans drink theirs lukewarm. Flavor is diminished with extremes of hot and cold. If you leave an orange on the counter the night before you eat it for breakfast, it will taste much better than if it were cold from the refrigerator. Cold beverages like

juice, iced tea, and milk are more flavorful when warmer than the icy temperature at which we are used to serving them. I am puzzled by the popularity of frozen candy bars; far fewer of the calories can be enjoyed than when the chocolate and caramel are at room temperature, or even slightly warmed. Scalding hot soups and beverages actually burn the tongue and inhibit taste at least until the damaged taste buds are replaced. In addition, the heat is so intense it overrides the more subtle sense of flavor. Rather than boil water to make hot chocolate, heat it to drinking temperature so there is less risk of burning and the drink can be rolled around in the mouth and truly tasted, rather than tossed down in quick sips with a grimace from the heat.

— Tasting the Good Life —

Expanding and enjoying the sense of taste requires breaking out of the phobia most of us have regarding food: unfamiliar equals bad. Many people grimace instantly when a new food is described or presented, even though they have no idea what it really tastes like. Don an attitude of curiosity, exploration, and open-mindedness, and have fun experimenting with your sense of taste.

Skin-Tasting

Right now, taste the back of your hand by placing your open mouth over it and gently swirling your tongue on the skin. Notice the clean, neutral taste of skin. You may get a pleasant, metallic

aftertaste from the trace of sweat that naturally exists. If you've ever had a bloody nose and tasted the blood as it ran down the back of your nose into the throat, you may find that skin tastes similar. Taste someone else's skin and see if you notice any difference.

Savoring Food and Drink

Whenever I see a particular friend, we get a pint of fine ice cream and split it. He eats his half within two minutes; mine easily lasts ten or more. He looks around for more as soon as he's done; I savor every molecule and sigh in contentment when I finish. You will enjoy food more if you savor it, like a wine taster savors each sip of wine. Here's how:

- When you drink something, take moderate sips and roll each one around all sides of your tonque. Notice how alive the taste is compared to merely letting it slide over the top of the tongue straight down your throat. Make sure the liquid is neither scalding hot nor ice cold for maximum flavor.
- Eat slowly, taking small bites. The more bites you take of food, the more surface area of the food will hit your tongue. Alternate bites of different foods, or take sips of a beverage between bites. Changing the tastes keeps the taste buds alert and expectant, whereas eating repeated bites of the same thing causes taste buds to desensitize.

- Smell your food before, and while, you eat. Smell is a far bigger factor in discerning and enjoying flavor than is taste.
- Feel the texture that determines much of our enjoyment: the rough feel of toast, the soft pillows of ravioli, the crisp apple and its juice sluicing around your mouth.

Teach Your Tongue

My parents enforced a simple rule at mealtime: to take at least one bite of everything so that our tongues would "learn to like it" (one brother was known for his amazing ability to split a pea in half, which qualified as his bite). The benefit of this "try everything" approach is that it begins familiarizing your tongue to varied tastes, which eventually builds to acceptance and enjoyment of those tastes. Research proves that repeated consumption of a food can increase preference for it, especially when consumed under pleasant circumstances and in the company of others who apparently enjoy those foods. Coffee is an example of an aversive taste taking on pleasurable aspects after repeated exposures to it; new coffee drinkers often use a lot of milk and sugar to temper the bitterness, and gradually eliminate those supplements as they grow to like the coffee taste itself. By "teaching your tongue" with the following tips, you can acquire such cosmopolitan tastes that you won't have to think twice about accepting dinner invitations based on what's being served, or eating at an Ethiopian restaurant where you've never tasted most of the items on the menu.

- Make a point of trying a small bite of each thing at a potluck, or ordering something you've never had before at a restaurant. I often split meals with the person I'm dining with: we decide together on two things and each eat half. That way we get variety. It's also a precaution if you're unsure that you'll like something; one of the meals can be something familiar and the other an experiment.
- Try making or ordering food from other cuisines: Greek, Afghan, Norwegian, Indian, Polynesian, or any of the many African cuisines such as Moroccan, Ethiopian, or Egyptian. Ask the wait-staff for recommendations. When I first tried sushi, the waiter suggested I start with one of the sweeter-tasting fish. I liked it, and then felt confident in progressing to more unusual tastes. The Yellow Pages of most metropolitan areas will list ethnic restaurants. The local city guide may also tell you where the people of a particular culture eat. There is a big difference between a real Mexican place and the Americanized version of Mexican food.

Glory in the Grocery

Once a week (or whenever you regularly visit the grocery) bring home a new, natural taste item. Many stores carry exotic fruits and vegetables that are worth the price at least once for fun. Food co-ops are especially good for non-mainstream foods, like amaranth and quinoa (pronounced keen-wa), high-protein grains that were widely grown by Central and South Americans until European rule all but stamped them out. Americans eat a very narrow range of all that is available, mostly since government and agriculture concentrate on just a handful of familiar foods.

Here's a few palate-stretching treats to look for. You'll find others as you explore.

- Fruits
    - ugli fruit
    - star fruit
    - papaya
    - pomegranate
    - mango
    - tangelo
    - kiwi
    - plantain
- Grains
    - quinoa
    - semolina
    - amaranth

- Beans
    - black
    - anasazi (ancient Native American bean)
    - soybean
    - adzuki (Japanese bean)

- Greens (all these are more nutritious than the traditional iceberg lettuce)
    - kale
    - romaine
    - red leaf lettuce
    - collards
    - mustard greens
    - beet greens
    - bean sprouts
    - alfalfa sprouts
    - wheat grass

- Vegetables
    - bok choy
    - kohlrabi
    - sunchoke (Jerusalem artichoke)
    - yam
    - nappa (Chinese cabbage)
    - turnip
    - parsnip
    - shiitake (Japanese mushroom)

- Canned items
    - water chestnuts
    - bamboo shoots

- Rice
    - basmati
    - wild rice
- Nut butters (alternative to peanut butter)
    - tahini (sesame butter)
    - almond butter
- Cheese
    - goat
    - feta
    - Camembert
    - Gruyère
- Herbs/spices
    - lemon grass
    - cilantro
    - sage
    - curry
    - turmeric
    - ginseng

Expand Your Definition of Food

Recently I heard someone telling a story of how iguanas are roasted in the Australian outback. Listeners automatically grimaced and exclaimed such things as "I'd rather starve!"

These people automatically shut the door on a food they had never tasted. However, lizards and snakes make very good eating

in many parts of the world; rattlesnake is even considered a delicacy in the western United States. During World War II, American pilots in the Pacific went hungry because they could not get themselves to eat lizards, strange sea creatures, toads, and insects, despite the fact they'd been taught that these were edible foods. People have a hard time eating something their society has labeled inedible. A survey commissioned by the United States Quartermaster Corps found forty-two different societies in which people eat rats; we shudder at the thought, yet colonial and modern Americans eat squirrel, a related rodent.

Keep your food definition door open. Be curious and consider every item eaten in the world as a valid food. Humans have evolved an enormous range of eating behavior; no other mammals, except rats and mice living in human settlements, possess the same ability to adapt to as many different conditions as humans. Take advantage of your evolution and be open to sampling, or at least mentally considering, things your culture does not define as food.

- Get the schedule of your local nature center and attend a natural food seminar. You may get the chance to try fungi and wild mushrooms (lightly fried in butter, they are delicious), fiddlehead ferns, dandelion greens, thimbleberries, rosehips, butternuts, spatterdock (lily pad root), cattails, acorn pancakes, or strawberry-leaf tea.

- Try edible flowers. Nasturtiums lend beauty and a peppery taste to salads; carnations have a gentle pungency.
- Eat the skins of fruits and vegetables. We are usually taught to throw skins away, yet they are often the most nutritious parts, and contain valuable fiber and roughage. They also taste good. As a child I would eat apple skins as fast as I could peel the apples for pie, finding the skins a special treat. Nibble on orange peel (or boil it and drink the citrus tea); savor the roasted taste of potato skin; munch the odd-looking skin of a kiwi. Try the white pectin that surrounds an orange inside the peel; turn your half a grapefruit inside out when you're done and eat the juicy membranes that divide each section (in our household this was required, both for the fiber, and to not waste a part of the fruit). Buying organically grown produce is wise, as the skin as well as the fruit of commercially grown produce holds some of the toxic pesticides. Buying food grown without artificial fertilizers, pesticides, and herbicides also helps support sustainable farming practices.
- Eat a wider variety of meats. If you are a meat eater, there is more to enjoy than muscle cuts. And there is more to the meat world than beef, chicken, and pork. Try goat, venison, or mutton for new flavors. Butcher shops sell organ meats that are delicious and highly nutritious: heart and

tongue look unusual, but are lean, smooth meats that are tasty hot or cold (excellent as sandwich meats onced cooked and chilled). Liver and kidneys are widely favored (the British especially prize beef and kidney pie). Giblets from poultry include heart, gizzard, and liver, and are good in soups, or breaded and fried. Some people enjoy "prairie oysters," the testicles of castrated cattle; a more widely accepted delicacy is ox tail, commonly made into soup. Bones from a ham or turkey make good bases for soup stock, as do chicken and turkey necks. Pickled pigs feet, head cheese (a jellied loaf containing meat from various parts of a pig), and tripe (stomach of ox) may be outside your culturization, but are enjoyed by many people and are probably available in your supermarket. Minnesotans prize walleye cheek, the tender chunk of meat on each side of the mouth of their state fish.

- Try your neighbor's weird food habits. Whether it be a peanut butter and pickle sandwich, raw cookie dough, pheasant, or stir-fried tofu and leeks, most food preferences are tasty. They may simply fall outside your narrow definition of what's good. I caught myself in the instinctive recoil from unfamiliar food when I learned about a food habit of a German community just seventy-five miles from where I live. There, in addition to common foods such as spaghetti, inhabitants like to eat blood

sausage. Not only was the food new to me, but also the unusual manner of eating it. The cook fries the blood sausage and keeps it hot (it turns black from the blood content when cooked). Diners lay both sides of their thick bread slices onto a plate of cream, put blood sausage on it, then drizzle it with corn syrup. My initial reaction was incredulity; then I realized that I enjoy those same tastes when I put both breakfast sausage and french toast on my fork, and swirl them in the syrup on my plate. I've now had blood sausage, eaten in the correct manner, and find it to be quite palatable. Thrifty farmers of every nationality save the blood from their slaughtered animals as a sausage ingredient. The Masai tribe of Africa bleed their cattle regularly, mixing the blood with milk for a protein-rich diet.

Listeners of the local morning public radio show in my city often request the song "Lime Jello Marshmallow Cottage Cheese Surprise." It is popular because it juxtaposes foods throughout the song that in no way seem to go together. But really, who knows until you try?

4

Hearing:
The Social Sense

Imagine your favorite person walking up to you, smiling and talking, and you cannot hear a word. You try to tell the person your problem, but without being able to hear your own voice, you quickly fall silent. The two of you look at each other, still friends, but at a loss as to how to communicate ideas and thoughts. You see children playing in the yard nearby, and cars speeding by, but the entire world has fallen absolutely silent. You perceive no sound.

Hearing is a profoundly social sense; the ability to communicate relies very much on hearing. Deaf people often find their condition isolating. Helen Keller, who was both deaf and blind, believed deafness was her greater loss, in that connecting with others was so difficult. Humans have created hundreds of complex languages that allow us to converse with, teach, and entertain each other. Every culture has given music a central role in all facets of life, from celebrating to mourning. For early humans, hearing was also essential to survival. A rustle in the forest led us to prey; a low growl warned us of danger nearby; a far-off rushing alerted us to a water source. Mothers the world over tune in to the particular cries of their child, distinguishing pain, hunger, or fear in an instant.

— The Amazing Ear —

Before you hear a sound it is magnified 200 times and transformed into five different forms of energy, all within a protected area in your ear not much larger than a hazelnut. Sound begins with the movement of any object, which bumps the air molecules next to it in motion. These molecules nudge their neighbors, which in turn push against others, creating an ever-widening surge of sound. Your outer ear scoops in these waves and funnels them into the ear canal, just ⅓-inch wide and one inch long, ending at the eardrum, a small, stiff membrane that moves when sound waves hit it.

This movement passes the action to your middle ear, home of the body's tiniest and most colorfully named bones: the hammer, the anvil, and the stirrup (or malleus, incus, and stapes). These function as a lever system that greatly amplifies the force of the vibrations transmitted by the eardrum. The first bone begins to move, its head fitting into the concave joint of the second, which then moves the third, which in turn presses against the tiny,

flexible window of the inner ear. This causes waves in the fluid of the cochlea, the snail-shaped organ of your inner ear. As the fluid passes over tiny hairs inside the cochlea, the hairs bend and excite nearby nerves that pass a signal on to the brain to be interpreted as sound. The rich neural or electrical network that supplies our tiny hearing system is large enough to supply a good-sized city with telephone service.

The fact that we hear is amazing considering the many transformations that take place before we interpret something as sound. Sound begins as acoustical energy in the air, and converts to mechanical energy when the hammer, anvil, and stirrup move. Mechanical energy changes to hydraulic when fluid of the inner ear receives the motion. Hydraulic energy becomes electrical energy as the cochlea hairs move and signal the nervous system. Electrical energy becomes neural energy as the auditory nerve passes it to the brain. And finally, neural energy becomes psychological energy as the brain interprets the impulse.

This path of membranes, canals, bones, and fluid is not the only way we hear, however. Some sound reaches us through bone conduction, the vibrations traveling through skull bones directly to the inner ear. You hear by bone conduction when you chew celery, click your teeth, and speak. In fact, because you hear your own speech through both bone and air, you sound much more powerful and dynamic to yourself than to your listeners. Your bone transmits rich, low-frequency vocal cord vibrations that are lost in the air, which is why when you hear yourself on tape your voice sounds thin. Despite its comparatively nasal and unfamiliar

sound, that's how your voice sounds to listeners, who only have the benefit of air conduction.

Test bone conduction right now: hold a ticking watch in your teeth and plug your ears. With all but the quietest watches, you will hear the ticking coming through your skull. My watch, which has just a faint tick when I put it to my ear, produces a musical clinking when I hear the tick through bone conduction. A cellist uses bone conduction by holding her tuning fork in her teeth to hear the pure tone she needs to tune her instrument amid the chaos of an orchestra warming up.

Your ears are connected to your throat by the eustachian tube, which regulates air pressure in the middle ear. Open only during chewing, swallowing or yawning, the eustachian tube ventilates the middle ear with air at the same pressure as the surroundings. That's why when you ascend or descend in an aircraft, chewing gum or yawning relieves the plugged feeling in your ears; the eustachian tube equalizes the air pressure between the air trapped in the middle ear and the air outside the eardrum. People with a cold are advised not to fly or scuba dive, as the inflammation in their throat may block the eustachian tube and spell disaster for their eardrum, which may rupture if pressure is not relieved. While the eustachian tubes are essential, they are also the Achilles' heel of the hearing system; middle ear infections are prevalent among humans, especially children, because of the connection to the throat.

— Do You Hear What I Hear?
The Nature of Sound —

All sounds are disturbances of the air vibrating out at various frequencies. The more rapid the vibration, or wave, the higher the pitch of the sound. Humans hear waves that vibrate anywhere from 20 to 20,000 cycles per second (cycles per second is also referred to as "hertz"). If hertz is thought of as the length of the wave, which would determine the number of waves that occur in a second, volume can be thought of as the height of the wave, or the amplitude (amplitude is often expressed in decibels, the smallest increments of sound a human ear can perceive). The greater the decibel level, the louder the sound. A sound with few cycles per second and high decibel level would be low and loud, such as the booming of thunder. Few cycles per second and low decibels would be like the soft, low groaning of an ice-locked lake. Similarly, high sounds can be as loud as the piercing of a jet engine or as soft as the peep of a baby bird.

The normal ear can distinguish some one million tones of various degrees of purity and complexity. The human ear perceives a wide range of sound, but it is only a sliver of all that is occurring. Our maximum of 20,000 hertz doesn't compare to a seal's aquatic hearing up to 160,000 hertz, or a cat, who hears up to 25,000 hertz. The whining and cringing of dogs for no apparent reason is often due to sounds we don't hear, as they pick up anything up to 35,000 hertz. In northern Wisconsin, where deer are plentiful and a danger to motorists at night, people mount tiny sirens on their vehicles that blast a sound too high for us to hear, but plenty of warning for animals.

Similarly, there are appliances that supposedly scare away spiders, who can hear only sounds above our range. If we heard higher frequencies than we do, we would have to plug our ears at night to shut out the myriad battle screams, clicks, and sirens of night insects, rodents, and bats. If we heard lower frequencies than we do, we could hear what elephants are saying but would also be inundated with the sounds of our body's internal workings. For example, plug your ears with both fingers; the low rumbling you hear is the contractions of muscles flexing and tensing in your arms and fingers.

Humans, as well as all other animals, are tuned to the frequencies most necessary for survival. Bats, who emit ultrasound (sounds higher than the human hearing range), are equipped to hear the echo of their sound bouncing off objects to locate their prey. They can pluck flying insects out of the air in total darkness. And some night moths, a principal food source for bats, not only hear the frequencies of bats, but produce their own ultrasonic sounds to confuse the predator, much as enemy air fighters jam each others' radars. It's lucky for us we cannot hear the racket; the volume of a bat's cries can reach 100 decibels, louder than a jackhammer on asphalt. Crickets scrape their wings together to communicate in an ultrasonic range; the chirpings we hear are just low, accidental bits of sound that happen to fall in our range. Were you to record a cricket's song and play it back, other crickets would not respond to it because the recording would have only picked up the part of their song that we can hear. It would be like listening to only the bassline of Beethoven's Fifth Symphony!

Crocodiles and elephants use infrasonics (sounds lower than the human hearing range). Humans were long puzzled by how elephants from miles around would know to come to the aid of a hurt, but seemingly silent, herd member. The desert-dwelling kangaroo rat has a greatly enlarged middle ear, enabling an incredible magnification of sound that allows it to hear the air passing over an owl's wing, and the scales on a striking snake rubbing together. The rat responds with a sudden high leap to escape the talons or the fangs. This sensitive ear is advantageous in the quiet desert; in any other environment, however, such acute ears would deafen the animal.

Sound occurs in any flexible medium that can conduct it—air, water, earth, even metals. Sound travels through air at 1,120 feet per second, significantly slower than the speed of light at 186,000 miles per second. This accounts for the delay between a flash of lightning and the thunder that follows, or for the bursting of fireworks before the sound of the explosion.

Sound travels faster through mediums other than air; steel conducts it at 16,500 feet per second, allowing you to get advance warning of a train coming by putting an ear to the steel rail. It travels through water at 4,200 feet per second, explaining why when swimming in the Mississippi as a kid, I would hear the clacking of a boat motor through the water as loudly as if it were about to overtake me, only to surface and find that the boat was far upriver and difficult to hear.

Some toothed whales use sound for hunting, emitting bursts of sound at decibels so high it kills fish and squid. Low frequency

sounds travel farther than higher, as you may have observed in hearing only the monotonous thumping bass from your neighbor's stereo. Fin whales take advantage of this fact, communicating across hundreds of miles of ocean at around 20 hertz, the lower limit of the human ear.

With so much to hear, we would be disabled by the processing of it all if our brains were not selective in what they pay attention to. In a noisy crowd we are able to focus on the speech of the person next to us, essentially ignoring the ocean of conversation going on all around. Yet we hear our name if it is spoken within earshot, and suddenly we are attentive to a conversation across the room. Parents become adept at going about their business while their children play outside, only to instantly notice an absence of or change in the sound. Our brain can detect differences of millionths of a second between when sound reaches the right and left ears, allowing for very accurate pinpointing of the source. Sound straight in front of you reaches the ears at the same time; any deviation from center results in a difference in when the sound reaches each ear, and the brain calculates the amount of difference to place the spot from which a noise came. Our ears are approximately six inches apart, so there is a time and volume difference in sound reaching one or the other. In addition, our head blocks the way for sounds to reach the far ear, creating a "sound shadow" that adds to our ability to place sounds.

On a hike in Minnesota's Voyageurs National Park I noticed a faint, unfamiliar scraping sound to my right. I stopped, turned to the right, and waited for the next occurrence. It came again,

low down, so I peered into the undergrowth. The next sound told me that it was about two feet from the trail, so I began scanning that area, still puzzled as to the source. Now it emanated continuously, but faintly, and I followed it in, guided and corrected by the sound like a horse by reins, until I discovered that it came from inside a downed tree limb: carpenter ants! Despite the muffled and diffused nature of the sound, my binaural hearing allowed me to zero in on it.

Many mammals have large external ears with muscles that allow them to aim at sounds without moving their heads. Often a cat will sit with its back to you, but have one ear turned back to keep track of your activity. Horses constantly swivel their ears in all directions, and dogs prick or flatten their ears frequently. Although fixed in place, our fleshy outer ear, the pinna, aids us in defining the height of a sound source, and whether it's in front or back of us. Depending upon the angle of sound waves reaching the ear, the contours of the pinna amplify different frequency bands as it sends sound into the ear canal. The brain uses these frequency cues to locate the sound.

The barn owl has the best hearing of any species tested, and is an expert in auditory localization even without an outer ear. Its ears are placed on each side of the head, like ours, and are also offset, one higher, and pointing upward, and one lower, pointing downward. This gives the owl more precise locating ability than a radar. From high overhead it is able to pinpoint the distance, direction, and elevation of the minute sounds of mice.

— Is That Music? —

Sounds can be roughly divided into the categories of speech, music, and noise. However, one person's music may be another's noise. Our categorization is very subjective. The perception of what is music changes with time and culture. Beethoven's later works were considered highly dissonant and unpleasant by listeners of the day, while contemporary audiences relish the music as some of the world's most beautiful. Much of modern orchestral music seems harsh and discordant because it employs more irregular rhythms and more unusual intervals of notes than we are used to. However, there may come a time when it is sought for its beauty.

Despite the ear's ability to distinguish minute differences in sounds, most cultures organize the vast range of audible sounds into musical scales of only five to seven notes. Each culture learns preferences for its own way of dividing the sound spectrum; Asian music with its subtle pitch changes sounds whining and off-key to Westerners because it uses smaller divisions between notes. Jamaicans prefer syncopated ballads, while Russians use lush minor melodies.

Music plays a prominent role in our lives; most people have an exquisite, inborn musical sense that develops subconsciously over their lifetimes. A baby responds to lullabies, and gravitates toward music. Pre-toddlers bounce to the beat of a song. We surround ourselves with music; before radios we sang as we worked and played, and in modern life we play music in our workplace, flip it on as soon as we get home, wake up to it, and play it in our

car. Music stimulates us. I always feel a surge of strength and adrenaline when speakers blast powerful music at the start of a ski race. Music makes exercise fun during classes at the YMCA, and has been instrumental in helping people enjoy exercise of all types. Most of our social occasions demand music, from a string quartet during a dinner party to a polka band at a wedding reception. Music enhances every party or sporting event. It's one way we mark an occasion as a celebration. The tingle of pleasure we can get from music releases endorphins—we are touched physically and emotionally by music.

Music also calms us down. In our increasingly stressful society, New Age-style music has become popular, with its amorphous melodies and lulling rhythms. It soothes us. Music therapy has emerged as its own discipline, with therapists trained to use music to reach mentally or physically disabled people. Classical music played in cardiac intensive care wards relaxes the patients. Psychotherapists have found music valuable in relaxing and reaching autistic children, who may find it easier to communicate in song than in speech. Massage therapists enhance their physical treatment with soothing music. Even comatose patients can respond to music. Many companies have installed "musical hold," a telephone feature that reduces a caller's perception of time on hold. Stores play music to help people linger, relax, and spend more money.

Our brains remember the relationships between notes, rather than the exact notes themselves. Most everyone can sing "Happy Birthday" starting on any random note. However, some people have perfect pitch, an exact memory of music that allows them to identify the key and names of notes in any song. Mozart

could remember an entire symphony after hearing it once. Even without perfect pitch, however, people can develop their musical sense into finer and finer dimensions.

My violin teacher's ear was so well developed that he didn't like listening to piano or guitar, instruments that produce "averaged" notes, a key or fret producing the same tone regardless of the music's context. His musical sense expected the same note to be played slightly differently depending upon the relationship of the notes before and after, much as letters in cursive writing differ slightly depending upon what letter precedes and follows them. String musicians tune their instruments by bowing two strings at once and listening for them to "pop" into perfect fifths, a sound the musician is trained to hear. Once my instructor walked in as I was tuning before a lesson for which I was unprepared, and in my nervousness I completely lost my sense of pitch and tuned the violin to fourths instead of fifths. It suddenly became a strange oriental-sounding instrument (and judging from the alarmed look in my teacher's eyes, not a pleasant one at that).

Singing is an expression of our musical sense. Cultures have songs for work, play, dance, entertainment, mourning, and ceremonies. An African saying sums up how natural singing is: "If you can walk you can dance, if you can talk you can sing." Recorded music has usurped our natural songs, inhibiting many of us to think we are not "good" enough. But infants create long, varied songs, children universally love to sing, and adults who give themselves the freedom enjoy singing immensely. When we sing, air passes over the vocal cords and causes them to vibrate.

Additionally, the bones and air spaces in our head vibrate. Close your mouth and hum; you'll feel your nose and teeth vibrating as sound passes through the skull straight to your inner ear. Singing causes our bodies to produce endorphins, natural "feel-good" drugs (sustained mantras for meditation are no accident).

Our natural bent toward singing helps us remember things if they are set to song: singing uses many parts of the brain, while speech uses only a small portion. When traveling I find that a guitar is the universal friend-maker. People instantly warm to music, and long to sing, especially now that creating our own music has been driven from our culture. Even when I cannot speak another person's language, I can touch and communicate with song.

Animals have their own music. Wolves in northern Minnesota will howl back to you over a frozen lake when you cup your hands and sing their song. The loon sends shivers up the spine with its maniacal laugh and long, mournful call. Humpback whales sing songs so haunting that their music has been made into best-selling recordings. During breeding season, the whales congregate and begin exchanging songs which may have up to eight themes, each one consisting of repeated phrases. The singing sessions can continue for up to twenty-two hours, with individual songs lasting from eight to twenty minutes each. The whales begin with themes from last year's songs, then gradually add, delete, and magnify them until all are singing a similar new song.

Courting fish crackle, grunt, purr, croak, and drum love songs that we can't hear, as our ears are not well adapted to a water environment. People can distinguish different groups of

killer whales by the different "dialect" of their sounds; similarly, birds of the same species will have slightly different songs in different regions.

Birds sing to establish territory, attract mates, and, we like to think, to give us pleasure. It is fitting that music flows naturally from animals and humans, as it has been found to follow a mathematical relationship that occurs repeatedly in nature itself. Musical variation falls midway between random and predictable, much as other natural patterns such as the growth of tree rings and the fluctuations in coastlines, mountain ranges, planetary paths, and water levels of the Nile. Perhaps the essential appeal of music is that it connects us intimately with the world.

— Ear Enemy No. 1: Noise —

Noise can be described as any undesirable sound. As society grows louder and louder, noise may best be described as any undesirable, potentially dangerous sound. Noise is the single greatest cause of hearing loss, more than all other causes combined. And hearing loss is the most common physical impairment in the United States.

We resign ourselves to the fact that hearing diminishes as one grows older; in our society a person has only a one in ten chance of normal hearing by age sixty-five. While at birth we may hear frequencies up to 30,000 hertz, our top range at age fifty is likely to be about 8000 hertz, and at age eighty is seldom more than 4000. Studies of a primitive African tribe that lives a quiet

existence have proven that, if used as nature intended, hearing can stay acute for an entire lifetime. However, we abuse it. Our world grows noisier every year.

You awaken to piercing beeps of your alarm clock. In the bathroom you flush the toilet, and use an electric shaver or hair dryer. You grind eggshells and fruit peelings down the kitchen disposal, while the dishwasher whines in the background. A radio blares the morning news, the blender screams, a TV babbles in another room. Baby bangs a cup on the tray, Joe drives up honking the horn of a car that needs a muffler. At work, you may have to put a meeting on hold while a jet goes by low overhead. You return to your desk where the phone jangles frequently. You immerse yourself in an echoing game of racquetball at lunch. After work you may mow the lawn, while the neighbor kids race mini-bikes up and down the street.

Noise began creeping into our society in the 1700s with the Industrial Revolution, and has been increasing steadily since. Our world teems with noisemakers that damage our ears: airplanes, trains, trucks, motorcycles. Even our recreation has become noisy, from water-skiing behind a powerful boat to snowmobiling, one of the most damaging activities both in intensity of noise and length of exposure. Thirty minutes behind a power lawn mower can exceed the noise safety measures recommended by the Occupational Safety and Health Administration (OSHA). Home power tools grow increasingly noisy. One vacuum manufacturer tried marketing a quiet model. People returned the machines, convinced the vacuum didn't work because it didn't make a lot of noise.

The damaging effects of noise are determined by intensity (volume, or decibel level), frequency, and length of exposure. Continued exposure to noise at more than 85 decibels is likely to lead to a loss of hearing. At 130 decibels, noise is painful. Let's compare some common sounds to these standards: Rustling leaves—20 dB; Average conversation—60 dB; Busy street with traffic—70 dB; Washing machine, dishwasher—75-78 dB; Motorcycle at 25 feet—90+ dB; Power mower—110 dB; Rock concert—100-130 dB; Shotgun blast—130 dB.

Noise above 85 dB affects our hearing by permanently damaging the tiny hairs in the cochlea. These hair cells do not regenerate, so each exposure to noise takes a little more toll on our hearing. We don't notice the damage for a long time, because it affects frequencies higher than we need to understand normal speech. But as the number of exposures to damaging noise increases, our upper threshold of hearing gradually lowers, until it begins to affect our perception of consonants, the higher-frequency sounds in speech that are essential to understanding it. Even a person with normal hearing may have trouble distinguishing between the letters 'b' and 'd,' 'f' and 's,' or 't' and 'd'; when hearing gets damaged enough, we lose even more and people sound as if they have furry tongues.

Many physiological changes are associated with noise. Stress reactions such as vasoconstriction (narrowing of the blood vessels) allow less blood to all the body organs, including the delicate ear. Without sufficient blood supply, cells inevitably degenerate, causing even further hearing loss. Noise increases aggressiveness

in children, retards learning, and contributes to birth defects. Even noise at low intensities can produce tension, anxiety, fatigue, or aggression. Think of the screech of chalk across a blackboard; squealing tires; continual ringing of a telephone; a song you dislike; a lone mosquito in your room at night; breaking glass. The stress of noise contributes to stress-related problems like migraines, ulcers, and high blood pressure.

— What's That Again?
Preserving Your Hearing —

There are habits you can create to help prevent hearing loss.

Avoid Noise

Shift into a quieter existence, or protect your ears when you are around noise. Flexible, putty-like earplugs available in drugstores filter out much damaging noise, and are advisable for anyone who regularly uses a noisy appliance, including lawn mowers, hair dryers, power tools, and electric razors. Every time you are around noise, see if you can reduce it. Try not to use the TV as background filler noise. When watching TV or listening to music, experiment with softer and softer volume. Over time this can actually sharpen your hearing. Do you really need to chop vegetables with a loud food processor? Can you run the dishwasher when no one is home? Is your car properly tuned and maintained,

running smoothly? Plug your ears carefully before using power tools, chain saws, lawn mowers, firearms. I wear earplugs when immersed in the raucous blare of aerobics class music, and in the weight room—the occasional sharp drop of metal weights has numbed my hearing temporarily when I did not wear plugs.

Eat a Low-Fat Diet

A high-fat diet clogs arteries and impairs blood circulation throughout the entire body. This damages the sensitive inner ear, which requires a fresh flow of blood to supply it with nutrients necessary to function. Interestingly, a deep crease in the earlobe is an indicator of heart disease, and is thought to be a local manifestation of hardening of the arteries. Studies bear out the adverse effects of a high-fat diet on hearing, and indicate that a low-fat, low-cholesterol diet may even reverse hearing loss caused by a high-fat diet.

Reduce Intake of Stimulants and Drugs

Caffeine, aspirin, alcohol, and tonic water (at least the quinine in it) are known to cause or aggravate hearing impairment. They may cause ringing in the ears and/or permanent hearing loss. There are other ototoxic (ear-damaging) drugs, especially antibi-

otics, but none as prevalent or as available as these. Avoiding stimulants like coffee or tobacco, and reducing use of drugs like aspirin and alcohol (especially drinks that have alcohol combined with tonic water) is not only good for your health, it's good for your hearing.

Relax

Stress damages your hearing along with most other parts of your body, and is the major trigger of many diseases. Reducing fatigue and tension will improve your entire being, including hearing.

Never Put Anything Smaller Than Your Knee in Your Ear

Children get beans stuck in their ears, but adults are no better. We have a penchant for sticking cotton swabs, bobby pins, or pencils down our ear canals, ostensibly to clean it, but in reality packing wax hard against the eardrum, limiting its movement, and in some cases damaging it. Cotton is the most common object doctors have to extract from adult ears. Leave ear wax alone; it is a lubricant designed to keep out foreign bodies like insects, dirt, and grime. In polluted areas, ears produce more wax as a defense against contamination. Wax starts as watery white droplets produced by sweat glands in the ear canal, and gradually solidifies into the sepia-colored wax we are familiar with. A few people are

genetically inclined to produce too much wax, and must have it removed regularly, but for the rest of us, wax dries up and drops out when we yawn, chew, or swallow.

— Hear Hear! —

Our hearing is a delightful sense to play with. The intentional use of hearing has not been proven to improve the physical sensing apparatus, but it does lower your hearing threshold by training the brain to make the most of what you hear.

Hearing from the Inside Out

There are a couple of exercises in bone conduction woven into this chapter. If you haven't tried them, do so now. Hold a watch between your teeth and plug your ears, to hear the tick come to your ears from inside your head. Also hum with your mouth closed, and feel the vibration in the entire front of your skull. Notice how noisy it is to eat crunchy things like carrots or chips. Then listen to someone else eat the same thing. The sound is a pale shadow of what you heard from inside your head.

The Shell and White Noise

Wordsworth wrote:

> *I have seen*
> *A curious child, who dwelt upon a tract*
> *Of inland ground, applying to his ear*
> *The convolutions of a smooth-lipped shell;*
> *To which, in silence hushed, his very soul*
> *Listened intensely.*

There is a certain amount of ambient noise all around us, much of it at frequencies we cannot hear. You can hear some of this by putting your ear to a conch shell (if you don't have a shell, use a coffee mug). You will hear sound resonating ("the sound of the ocean" we tell children), with the main frequency going down the closer the shell is to your ear. Move the shell or cup away slowly and hear the sound go up.

"White noise" is a random combination of all frequencies, and is often soothing to people. Companies play white noise over the speaker system on the floor housing computer programmers, who need to concentrate. The sound isn't consciously heard, but has a calming effect. Many people need a fan to get to sleep, because the even, constant noise muffles other distractions.

Voice It

Bend both ears forward with cupped hands, and talk. Notice how different your voice sounds; sharper, higher, crisper. You are hearing it a little more as your listeners do. Another way to do this

is to face tightly into a corner and talk. The two walls will bounce your voice back. For the truest sense of what you sound like, record your voice and play it back. Without the low-frequency sounds that you hear internally when you speak, your recorded voice will sound higher than what you're used to.

Silence is...Impossible

Composer John Cage wrote a piece called "4'33." The pianist walks out on stage, and takes her seat at the piano. She sits for a moment, appearing to center her mind before playing, like a gymnast pauses before a routine. She sits. And sits. The audience gets nervous: Does she have stage fright? Is she okay? People begin to move uncomfortably, clear their throats, rustle their fabrics. There's a siren faintly outside. A giggle from the back row. The constant whishing of the air conditioning. The squeak of a chair. An airplane overhead. Breathing. The zip of a purse. And gradually, the audience comes to understand that the piece is being played — by the world. By requiring the performer to not make a sound for four minutes and thirty-three seconds, the composer gets the audience to listen. Cage said, "The purpose of this purposeless music would be achieved if people learned to listen. Then when they listened they might discover that they preferred the sounds of everyday life to the ones they would presently hear in the physical program.... That was all right as far as I was concerned."

There is sound all around us, all the time. Even deep in the woods, at night, where at first it is so quiet that ears seem full of one's own body sounds, there is sound. Trees whisper and speak as the wind caresses them. An owl hoots a hollow call. Thunder rolls far in the distance. Try enjoying all the sound you hear when it is "quiet." This first requires that you not add any sound. Give the stereo and television a break, and go about your tasks. I prefer quiet now that I have become accustomed to it. Now I find it irritating to have the babbling of television or radio in my space. We cannot achieve total silence without a specially designed room, and those who experience absolute silence find it disturbing. But quiet has a gentle hum to it of everyday sounds. I find it soothing and pleasurable, something I look forward to.

Gee, This Food Sounds Good!

Some foods have irresistible sounds. If you tune in to the sound of food you will enjoy it in yet another dimension. Here are some of my favorite food sounds. Start noticing your own.

- Macaroni and cheese, stirred slowly (luscious clicking sound)
- The pop and sizzle of frying fish
- Rising musical question when pouring liquid into a cup
- Soft snap of saltine on its perforation

- Crunch of a carrot
- Delicate, muffled tearing of fresh spinach leaves
- Cleaving snap of crisp apple
- Crinkly crack of eggshell against a bowl
- Gulping mud-pot plop of hot cereal cooking
  on the stove

Musical Sampler

Like your tongue, your ears must be trained to expand their world. Sample types of music you are unfamiliar with, listening with curiosity and openness. I occasionally walk my way through stereo channels and listen for a short time to Latin, then classical, then pop, then rap, then big band to expand my experience and appreciate the variety of musical modes.

Music theorist Leonard Meyer of the University of Pennsylvania proposed in the 1950s the now-popular notion that the enjoyment of music comes from a subtle interweaving of expectation and surprise. New genres of music may contain too much surprise for you to enjoy them at first, but as you gain some familiarity you will build enough expectation to make the balance right. Often a classical piece seems long and involved at first, but after several hearings, a listener comes to look forward to each melodic twist: festive trumpets, plaintive oboes, or the sonorous

entrance of the cellos. There may be styles you can't come to like, but at least you can dislike them knowledgeably.

I was asked to play strolling violin for a prom dinner, and when I asked the mother of the prom-goer about the kind of music he liked, she said he really only listens to heavy metal. I groaned inwardly. Heavy metal is one style of music I felt I could never like. I asked for a couple of tapes, figuring that perhaps I could glean a melody here and there. As it turned out, I actually liked some of the songs, and when I played one during the dinner it was quite a hit. Listening and giving it a chance opened my mind.

Take Music Apart

When you've had enough exploring, take three minutes to listen to all the parts in music you already enjoy. Listen for the lowest notes; try to follow the bass line of a song. Identify the percussion that adds body to everything but rarely gets noticed: a soft cymbal roll, a ting of the triangle, the vibrating thump of a bass drum. Mostly our ear follows the highest notes, and they are often the melody. Try to hear what's buried in the middle and beneath.

This is difficult to do until you've had practice. I first started to notice finer nuances when I participated in a commercial recording session. The song was laid down track by track, and with each subtle addition, the entire sound was enhanced. A tiny tap on the snare livened it up; adding a third vocal in one place made the whole thing sound rich; dotting a faint line of a high

synthesizer added excitement. Without having heard the music take form, I never would have noticed those things. Even when trying to hear them, they were hard to notice as they melded in with the whole.

Sing

Virtually all people, even the many who claim they "can't sing," find joy in singing. Witness the prevalence of shower singers, and notice all the people who rock their heads and sing in their cars. We as human beings love to sing. Modern society has made little room for it, but people still find an outlet at churches, where the anonymity of a crowd makes it easier. My mother plays for songfests at a nursing home. The old-time melodies stimulate memories, arouse latent emotions, provide camaraderie, and produce wonderful tales to share. Community and church choirs proliferate, as people want and need an outlet for musical expression.

Sing at home; with your children; in the shower. Take long walks and sing with exuberance. Singing makes you breathe deeply, involves both lobes of your brain, releases feel-good endorphins, and is just plain fun. Involve your body in the internal massage that is singing.

Make a Sound List

Just for fun, list the sounds you really like. You'll be surprised at what pleases you once you think about it; for example, I like hearing people's shoes click, creak, and grind as they walk on a sidewalk. The tinkling of water when I splash my face. A burbling brook. The electronic bump of my stereo when I turn it on. The crackling of spreading butter on toast. The click of computer keys. Notice and enjoy the tiny auditory pleasures that surround you.

5

Vision:
The Dominant Sense

Humans are predators; the eyes prove it. Just like the eyes of lions, wolves, owls, and other hunters, our eyes face forward to provide detailed depth perception vital to judging distance and recognizing objects. Our typical prey, such as a rabbit or deer, has eyes on each side of the head so that it can see broadly in all directions, albeit with less depth and detail.

While human eyes were designed for such things as spotting prey, scanning the horizon for weather, and keeping track of active children, they have become far more than simply a survival tool. Vision stimulates thought and provides life enrichment. Even prehistoric humans painted pictures to express themselves visually. Eyesight dominates the human senses: 90 to 95 percent of all our sensory perceptions

are visual, and over 80 percent of what we learn comes to us visually. The brain devotes almost four times as much space to vision than to touch, and ten times more than for hearing.

Our eyesight has a broad range. We can thread a needle inches from our eye, and from a mountain peak on a clear, moonless night see a match struck fifty miles away. We use vision to discern and appreciate beauty, ponder the universe as we view stars and planets, read complex languages we've created, and catch balls as we play games.

Visual images are natural means to enhance learning. Chemical formulas, planetary patterns, dance steps, and basketball plays all become clear upon seeing a diagram. Vision plays a vital role in communication, as more than 60 percent of communication consists of nonverbal, visual cues. Sexual attraction relies greatly on vision. Our upright stance displays sexual organs, and our species even has the unique ability to copulate face to face. Poets, writers, and lyricists hold the eye in high regard as a "window to the soul," and often rhapsodize on the beauty of the eye itself.

The human visual system is the most complex in the world, thanks to the large brain that can make meaning out of all a person sees. Our sight takes place not in the eye, but in the brain, which allows us to dream, imagine, and remember images. While a hawk sees four times more detail than we do, being able to spot a mouse from a half-mile in the air, its eye weighs more than its brain and functions purely for survival. The human eye, versatile and highly accurate, can shift focus in a split-second from a newspaper in hand to an airplane miles above. It can adapt in seconds from a dark basement to the dazzling bright of day,

distinguishing some one million combinations of color hue, saturation, and brightness, and estimating distance, size, and movement of objects.

— What's in an Eye? —

Though our dominant sense, vision develops last prenatally, and functions the least well of all our sensory systems at birth. Within the first few days of life a newborn can distinguish shapes and patterns, and can follow a slowly moving object. However, we do not achieve accurate, detailed vision until about age seven.

We quickly notice people's eyes, and we make judgments based upon them. Shifty eyes make a person seem sneaky and dishonest; "doe eyes" give the impression of naiveté; "bedroom eyes" with their lowered lids connote sexuality. Set inward under brow and cheek bones for protection, the eye gains shadow and depth, which augment its beauty.

Eyelids reflexively blink every two to ten seconds to keep the eye cleansed with tears, but also aid in the vast array of expressions, from surprise to anger to love. Lashes shade the eye, adding to its mystique as well as catching sand and debris (although ours cannot match the luxurious four-inch eyelashes of the desert-dwelling camel).

Inside the eye itself, under the clear cornea, lies the iris, from the Greek word for rainbow, which gives the eye its color. The ice greys, crystal blues, sea greens, jeweled hazels, and rich browns of human eyes come from pigments in the iris which absorb parts of the light spectrum and scatter back the rest. Eyes with little

pigment reflect back a lot of light, including the short blue end of the spectrum, and appear blue. Brown eyes, endowed with lots of pigment, absorb all but the long waves toward the red end of the spectrum, and appear brown. The iris often has spots, patterns of color, or starburst designs, all of which are as individual as a fingerprint.

The center of the iris is a hole, the pupil, which appears black because of the darkness of the eye within. The pupil can open to as large as a pencil eraser to gather more light under dim conditions, and constricts to pinhead size when under bright light.

However, it also indicates emotions, enlarging whenever we view something of interest. In studies, men shown a picture of an attractive, bikini-clad woman responded with larger pupils. Similarly, men shown two photographs of a woman, the second with the pupils retouched to look larger, rated the second photo as more appealing even if they did not consciously discern the difference in the two, perhaps because in the second picture the woman appears interested in them.

Ancient Chinese jade sellers would watch a prospective buyer's pupils as he looked over several pieces. When the pupils enlarged, the seller knew which piece the buyer fancied and could set the price accordingly. Experiments have shown that when a hungry person sees a picture of appetizing food, the pupils open wider.

Just inside the pupil lies the lens, a flexible mass of transparent sheets in an elastic case, held by muscles. Unlike a camera lens, which moves toward or away from the target to focus, the human lens remains stationary. It changes its shape to focus. If the object of interest lies far away, the lens relaxes into its natural

thin, flattened shape. When the viewer desires near focus, the lens thickens and contracts. Our lens cannot bulge enough to focus underwater, but we can gain clear images in water by imposing air between it and our eye, as with a scuba mask. Many aquatic animals, such as seals, cannot flatten their lens enough to see well in air.

Whether looking near or far, the lens accommodates to focus light onto the back of the eyeball, the retina. This thin sheet contains cells connected directly to the brain's visual cortex, and are thought of as an extension of the brain itself. Two kinds of cells abound in the retina. The thin, straight rods, numbering 130 million, report only in black and white, and come into play in low light. Owls, cats, and other nocturnal animals have only rods, and thus do not sense color. This is true for most diurnal mammals as well, including the bull, who wouldn't know if the matador's cape was red or black. Seven million plump cones specialize separately in blue, red, and green, and combine to show us the myriad colors of the day, as they do for birds, insects, reptiles, and fish. They are concentrated mostly in a one millimeter crater at the back of the retina, called the fovea.

Here our lens targets light as it focuses, for only here can a human see clearly. Not only is the density of cells great, but here each cone has a nerve going directly to the brain. In other parts of the retina, the cones are bunched into groups, each group sharing one nerve cell to the visual cortex. This "sweet spot" of clear vision manifests itself on the outside as a spot about four inches square at eight feet. The closer in it is, the smaller the spot.

The human fovea is centrally placed and circular in shape, the same as other animals that inhabit forests and other visually

137

complex settings. Animals that need to see a broad range, such as grazing animals of the African bush, tend to have an elongated, horizontal fovea. Birds of prey, some of the keenest-sighted animals in the world, have three foveas; an elongated strip to see the horizon, and two deep pits in each retina that act as telephoto lenses, magnifying the images that fall upon it. Insects see clearly across their whole range of vision because each of the tiny units of their compound eyes has a fovea.

Everything perceived by cells outside our fovea registers as softly blurred. Peripheral vision with its mixture of rods and cones gives us a broad, but fuzzy, sense of what's out there. We're not aware that we see only one spot clearly at a time because our eyes constantly jump around. We couldn't hold them still if we tried. Researchers have tracked eye patterns of subjects who were asked to stare at a small dot. While the subject believed his eyes never wavered, in truth they minutely skipped and jerked all around the object. This same skipping-gaze phenomenon causes us to believe that a candle flame in a dark room is moving around.

The very edges of our retina contain only rods, the source of our night vision. In dim light, our pupil widens to allow more light, and the lens dutifully focuses the light on the fovea, but to no avail, as the cones there require a lot of light to create the chemical reaction that allows color sensation.

However, the rods spring to life with the low light levels. Since rods are more dense along the edges of the retina, our peripheral vision becomes better than our central vision as the light fades. Our overall vision reaches its nadir at twilight, when

neither the rods nor cones are working at peak efficiency. Twilight motorists may fail to see a bicyclist on the edge of the road, or a raccoon crossing the road—neither the central nor peripheral vision has clear focus.

Once night falls, however, the rods are working fully. Try this: look directly at a star; it seems to disappear, yet when you look away from it you see it easily.

When you see pairs of eyes glowing in the night you are viewing a nocturnal animal, such as a cat or rabbit, which has a reflective layer behind the retina that bounces light out again to give the rods a second chance to absorb the rays. In very low light, humans lose all color sensation as the cones cease to function. A red shirt will look black, a yellow flower will look white, and colors in between will be various shades of gray. Even during the day our peripheral vision senses light and dark, and signals us to whirl our head and focus on any movement that may be meaningful, whether it be a dark shot of an insect in the house or the flash of skin as someone comes up from behind.

One spot on the retina lacks rods and cones, where the optic nerve is attached. Because our eyes move constantly, we never really "see" this blind spot. Additionally, one eye sees a slightly different view from the other, and each blind spot will occur in a different spot on the visual field, so the other eye covers the blank. We can be fooled, though, and many an accident has been caused by a driver truly not seeing another vehicle.

You can demonstrate your blind spot by drawing two black spots the size of a pencil eraser on a sheet of paper. Make them

about three inches apart. Now cover your left eye with one hand, and look at the left dot with your right eye. Keeping the left eye covered, move the paper slowly toward your face as you stay focused on the left dot. At a certain point you will cease to see the right dot, while moving the paper a bit forward or backward from this spot will reveal it. You have hit the blind spot when the dot disappears.

In absence of information from the other eye, the brain fills in whatever background is most likely to be there; in this case, the color of your paper. If a softball lying in the grass falls on your blind spot, your brain will fill the spot with green grass.

— Vital Light —

What we call light is only a tiny portion of the huge spectrum of electromagnetic energy which encompasses wavelengths as large as the distance from Earth to the sun (such as the resonating frequency of Earth) to wavelengths roughly the diameter of an electron (caused by cosmic rays such as those from solar flare-ups). Humans see only wavelengths of 400 to 700 nanometers (millionths of a millimeter), which we perceive as deep blue to deep red. Wavelengths below this are called infrared, and we can perceive a narrow band of them as body heat. However, snakes easily see infrared and can spot their prey in total darkness. Below infrared wavelengths are the waves used to carry television and radio signals, and lower still is the miniscule range humans perceive as sound. Just above our visible spectrum is ultraviolet

light, which causes suntanning and kills germs. With all this energy vibrating and pulsing, it is no wonder that all creatures evolved to perceive only the part of the bombardment necessary for survival in their niche of the world.

The origin of sight stretches back 300 million years, to ancient sea creatures that developed faint patches of thin skin sensitive to differences in dark and light. As life forms increased in complexity, eyes evolved that could tell the direction from which light came, then detect motion, then form, then detail, then color. Perhaps as a reminder of these origins, our eyes now must be continuously bathed in saltwater.

Just as some animals, such as snakes, can see part of the spectrum below our perception, many creatures see ultraviolet light that is above our range. Birds see ultraviolet light and can orient their flight to the sun even on dark days. Bees do not see the low reds on our spectrum, but see well into the ultraviolet range. Therefore, a flower's bright red bloom will be essentially invisible to a bee, although the ultraviolet pattern in it will be visible to a bee and not to us. Two red flowers may be as different as blue and yellow to a bee. A white flower appears blue to a bee, while some trees look magenta, and some green plants glow red. Fish that inhabit the deep oceans are sensitive only to the blue hues of the ambient light, while goldfish have a remarkable range from infrared to ultraviolet. If humans could sense the same radiation as the goldfish, we would see the remote control beams that operate television and videos, and an office building would be illuminated by the infrared light from security cameras.

Sunlight is "white" light, comprising all of the visible spectrum as well as infrared and ultraviolet. In 1666, Sir Isaac Newton discovered this by passing sunlight through a prism, which separated it into its component colors, then passing that spectrum through another prism, which reunited the colors to white light. Nothing in the world has color: light is the only source of color. All the colors we see are simply relections of part of the spectrum. Pigments are absorbers, reflectors, or transmitters of light. The green in the leaves of trees comes from chlorophyll, the substance that converts sunlight into food through photosynthesis. Chlorophyll absorbs most of the short end of the spectrum, the blues and purples, and most of the long red waves at the other end. Green and a little red remains, which are reflected back to our eyes. As autumn signals the chlorophyll to retreat, different colors emerge as the pigments underneath absorb and reflect different parts of the spectrum. Red shoes are red only because the dye absorbs all waves of the spectrum except red. Your favorite black sweater absorbs all wavelengths and reflects no color at all. Polar bear fur scatters back all wavelengths of light, which together form white.

Pigments look different under different lights, because they still absorb or reflect parts of the available light spectrum. Human skin becomes greenish under mercury lights, which lack the longer, "warmer" wavelengths that our skin reflects from sunlight. A book that appears red in daylight will be black under green light, because green light does not contain the one color, red, that can be reflected. Paper that is white in daylight becomes blue under blue light, and red under red light, because it reflects back all the light that reaches it.

Were there no dust or gases in the sky, the heavens would appear black even at midday. However, Earth's atmosphere contains gases whose molecules scatter the light. Because they scatter the blue end of the spectrum, the short wavelengths, more than they do the longer wavelengths, the sky looks blue to us. Dust or moisture particles scatter some of the longer wavelengths as well, and cause the sky to appear whiter (notice how much lighter the sky is near the horizon compared to the deep blue straight above; at the horizon you are looking through more atmosphere, with more gases to scatter a wider spectrum of light).

Mercury's sky is black, Venus' gray, Mars' pink because different gases in their atmospheres scatter a different band of frequencies. Our sunset takes on brilliant warm colors because the sun's light pierces through more miles of atmosphere near the surface of the Earth; as its angle becomes lower, increased dust and moisture reflect the longer, red wavelengths. Thus, the light may begin as yellow, deepen to orange, and diminish in an intense, red blaze.

— Two Eyes, One Scene —

Human eyes are most closely related to the other primates such as apes and monkeys, who require detailed color vision to spot fruit and prey in a jumbled environment and excellent depth perception to judge shapes and distance as they swing through trees. Depth perception comes from the overlapping of two fields of vision. This makes the overall range of vision narrower, but

receiving two images of the same scene provides greater detail, and improves perception in poor light.

A rabbit's two visual fields overlap 24 degrees, while ours overlay a full 180 degrees. The pupils of our eyes are about two-and-a-half inches apart, so each eye has a slightly different angle on the world. You can easily see this by closing this book and holding the spine toward you; alternate closing first one eye, then the other. Each eye will see the spine and a little of only one of the covers. By combining the flat images from both eyes, the brain achieves perspective of a three-dimensional book.

I wear contact lenses, and sometimes out of curiosity look around using only one lens. With one eye very blurry and the other clear, I can see how my brain mixes the two images. Muscles attached to our eyes aim them both at the same point, even if one eye is blindfolded, while some animals, like the seagull and chameleon, can move their eyes independently and see two different scenes. The owl's eyes take up one-third of its head and are so large that they do not move at all, but its head swivels to see 360 degrees. The squirrel's eyes evolved near the top of its head to allow an upward range, to watch for hawks while running on the ground, and to look back over its head and down its spine to check for pursuers while running up a tree.

Although we are unaware of it, we see double of everything except what's in our small area of focused vision. Look around the room right now, and notice the two blurry noses at the bottom of your field of vision. We see our nose, doubled, all the time, but tune it out because the images are far apart and fuzzy. Here's

another example of double vision: hold your right forefinger about twelve inches in front of your face, and the left forefinger out front as far as you can reach. Focus on the left finger (without straying) and notice that you have suddenly sprouted an extra right forefinger. As long as you are watching the more distant finger, the closer one is doubled. Now switch your focus to the right, closer finger, and see how the left one is doubled. Although stereoscopic vision causes us to see double all the time, our brain interprets it as one scene.

— Now You See It; Now You Don't —

If a bee were trapped in a cinema, it would see a series of still images, and 50 percent of the time it would see a blank screen. The bee's "critical fusion" is far higher than ours. Critical fusion refers to the phenomenon of an image remaining on the retina for a fraction of a second. If another image occurs during this time, we perceive no interval between the two and they appear continuous. In bright light we can perceive sixty images per second. In low light, fewer than ten.

Movie theaters are darkened to lower our critical fusion frequency, so films consist of twenty-four frames per second and appear continuous to us. Bees and flies can see 300 images a second, an advantage for such fast-moving creatures. Were we to see images with such quick resolution, all our electric bulbs would flicker because of the alternating current. Fluorescent lights appear to throw constant light, but are really flashing off and on

like strobes. You notice this when the frequency slows down, as when a bulb gradually dies.

Nocturnal insects have a low critical fusion frequency because they need more time to gather light from an image. The cricket, for example, sees forty-five images per second. I vividly recall a ten-minute run down the sloping, rugged trail from Locater Lake in Minnesota's Voyageur National Park, in which I felt my eyes grabbing images at maximum speed to tell my body how to react; how high to jump to clear that log, how far to swing each leg to land on the irregular places that looked to be solid footholds. Athletes of fast-paced games such as basketball rely on their ability to perceive what's going on as quickly as possible.

Our brains cleverly piece together bits of information, and even fill some in, so we can "see" what may be invisible. A human can see a telephone wire from over a quarter mile away, while it is barely visible in photographs. We see things well that we are practiced in noticing—our minds hold a memory bank of visual data. Children visually stimulated with unusually-patterned toys and mobiles develop increased ability to learn. Lack of visual stimulation results in reduced perception; kittens raised in a room containing only vertical lines develop normal vertical vision, but cannot perceive horizontal lines, and vice versa.

When I am looking for wildlife on a hike, my eager but city-trained eyes see a deer in every horizontal brown log; yet a trained Alaskan guide picks mountain sheep out of matching rocks from miles away. The whitewater kayaker reads the water as precisely as the pianist reads music.

Artists use the eye's ability to fill in detail. Picasso drew a single line to give a hint of a woman's form, leaving the viewer to fill in a body. The eye easily interprets a painter's flurry of greens and browns to be a forest, or a sculptor's single molded wire to connote entwined lovers.

Our brains fill in color in our peripheral vision, even though we actually perceive it poorly or not at all. You can demonstrate this by having a friend slowly bring an unidentified object into your peripheral vision while you look straight ahead. You will see the object at the edge of your vision, but not interpret the color until it is closer to your main visual field. However, once you know its color, you will "see" it all the way through your peripheral vision as the object moves out again.

Humans demonstrate "color constancy," which means that once we know the color of something, we always see the color even when we truly can't perceive it. A red car will appear red to its owner in virtual darkness, when really she is seeing it as black or dark gray. We perceive a cardboard box as uniformly brown even if it is half lit by sunlight and half in shadow. However, sometimes the brain abandons color constancy; if you present a broiled steak under blue light it will look putrid, even though the diner knows the color of the steak. Humans are programmed from birth to recognize faces; so strong is this patterning that we see faces in the moon, rocks, and houses (windows and doors often appear to be eyes, nose, and mouth).

Human eyesight does have limitations. For example, our brains persists in assigning a top, bottom, and sides to things.

Babies often fail to recognize a familiar object if it is simply turned a different direction. Even as adults, we don't recognize an outline of the United States tipped on its eastern seaboard, nor familiar faces when photographs are turned upside down.

Subjects in an experiment wore goggles that turned everything upside down. It took two weeks for them to stop reaching up to tie their shoes, or stepping up to go down stairs. However, their brains did adapt to the new world, eventually allowing them to ride a bike and even ski. After several weeks, the glasses were removed, and the subjects had to go through another adjustment period to get used to the world right side up.

The brain always assumes that light comes from above, and we get confused when it doesn't (in a typical spookhouse trick, someone shines a flashlight on his face from below; the ghastly result registers as other-worldly). Similarly, we cannot recognize faces when light and dark are reversed, as in a photograph negative. Stuart Anstis, a perceptual psychologist at the University of California at San Diego, plunged himself into the negative world with a pair of glasses that reversed black and white, and converted colors to their complements, such as blue to yellow and purple to green. People became black-toothed, shadows appeared as white ghosts, and meals took on surreal colors, such as blue scrambled eggs. In three days, his brain adapted very little; another person tried for eight days and found the same. Certain rules seem to be "hard-coded" into the brain.

Vision, like most other senses, degenerates if not stimulated. If you roll a sheet of paper into a tube and stare through it at a

solid-colored plane, the color will eventually fade to neutral gray. Additionally, we are subject to many optical illusions; we perceive straight lines passing through a curved pattern as bent, we think a vertical line is longer than a horizontal line of the same length (a drawing of a top hat proves this; the vertical part of the hat intersects the horizontal brim and makes the brim appear shorter). We see an oasis of water in the distance on a hot, landlocked highway because heat radiating upward from the ground reflects back the sun's light before it hits the ground. The light rays carrying scattered blue light from the sky bend, and we see the blue of the sky wavering on the roadway.

— Clues to Perception —

Even people with vision in only one eye have some depth perception, thanks to monocular visual clues. With increasing distance, the detail of line and texture decrease. For example, a plowed field looks rough and cloddy up close, but smooth and even in the distance. Cobblestones are distinct nearby, with clear definition between each of them, but meld into a solid pavement farther away. The ornate pattern of an Oriental rug melts into an indistinct rippling at the far end of a hallway. A similar smoothing of detail occurs when viewing rows of cereal boxes at the grocery.

Relative size and color are additional clues to depth. We know that a train in the distance is full-sized, even though in our vision it may be as small as a toy, because of other size cues

around it; trees, buildings, and landscape allow us to compare unfamiliar things to familiar, helping us judge size and distance. Color clues us, since nearby objects tend to be brighter; distance mutes colors. A range of mountains dramatically displays this principle. Those in the foreground are clear, detailed, colorful, and larger; progressively distant ranges take on increasingly muted tones, and those furthest in the distance are pale blueish shapes.

Horizon gives us yet another clue to depth, for we see the horizon as higher than the ground upon which we stand, such as when we look out to sea. Therefore, objects higher and smaller in our field of view are seen as farther away. Lines we know to be parallel, such as the edges of a highway, converge at a point on the horizon, another clue to depth.

— What Affects Vision? —

The quality of our vision changes from moment to moment; a person with confirmed 20/20 vision (sees at twenty feet what the average person sees at twenty feet) may at some times worsen to 20/40 vision (sees at twenty feet what a normal person sees at forty feet), and other times may display acuity of 20/15. Age changes vision, as lens fibers constantly generate throughout our lives, gradually thickening the lens and making it less able to contract to accommodate near vision. The lens of an eighty-year old measures 50 percent larger than that of a twenty-year old.

Consider that at the turn of the century, the average American's lifespan was forty-seven years, and now it exceeds seventy-

five. We are simply using our eyes much longer. Daily changes in conditions also affect our vision. Our eyes adjust in split seconds from dark to light, but take several minutes to adjust from bright to low light. Have you ever tried to find a seat in a darkened theater after coming in from the bright lobby? While our eyes do get somewhat accustomed to the darkness within a minute or two, full adaptation to dark takes up to sixty minutes. Occasionally I will turn off all the lights and light a candle; at first the room seems very dark, and the candle light very low. After a while my eyes fully adjust, so that I can easily write letters by the light and see detail around the room. Perhaps it was not such a hardship to have worked by candlelight before the invention of artificial light.

Artificial light is both a blessing and a curse when it comes to our eyesight. While it prevents us from straining to see by illuminating our work areas and homes with high light levels, it also divorces us from the natural "light clock" of the sun. Sunlight affects our sleeping and waking cycles, hormones, growth, sexual maturation, body temperature, moods, and appetite. We spent millions of years adapting to natural light, and now spend almost all our waking hours under artificial light spectrums (in schools, offices, and homes) which do not substitute for the sun. Before the advent of artificial light, we went to bed when the natural light faded, and arose as the sun nosed into the sky each morning. Our eyes had plenty of time to rest. Now, however, we use our eyes intensely all day, then come home and relax by reading or watching television, often until bedtime. The extension of our day

causes eye strain, which many believe causes deteriorating vision (more than 50 percent of Americans wear corrective lenses, and the number seems to be on the rise).

Our eyes are designed for distance; in their relaxed state they naturally focus as if looking for a deer across the field. Throughout most of human history we spent little time on near-point tasks such as cooking or making weapons. It has been only in the past century or so that vast numbers of people in developed countries began spending the better part of their days doing paperwork, reading, and assembling small parts in factories.

It is only in the past decade that millions of us have become glued to computer screens. The implications for our vision are sobering. Eyes designed for seeing far away continually focus close in. Glare off computer screens, white paper, and desk tops further strains the eye. Our bodies were designed for action, and the sedentary jobs that require prolonged computer use reduce circulation and aerobic capacity, both of which have an effect on our eyes. In short, we need to give our vision special attention to help counteract the effects of our unnatural use of eyes and body.

— How to Develop Eagle Eyes —

The following tips and exercises will guide you on the road to developing or maintaining sharper vision.

Reduce Stress

Mental and physical stress constrict the blood vessels, directly reducing blood flow to the oxygen-dependent retina. In some cases, errors of refraction, which cause people to have poor vision such as near- or far-sightedness, can be corrected by the reduction of mental strain that keeps the lens from focusing correctly. Visual therapists and behavioral optometrists specialize in training people to alter and improve their vision by reducing stress, training eyes to work properly, and improving diet, work organization, and general health. Try these simple vision therapy exercises during the day:

- *Palming* relaxes the visual system, helps neutralize stress, eyestrain, and headache. Support your elbows on a telephone book or other comfortable surface, and cup your hands over your closed eyes so no light gets in. The heel of your palm should rest on your cheekbones, and your fingers cross on the forehead. Put no pressure on the eyes themselves. Breathe slowly and deeply, and imagine some wide-open setting such as a tropical ocean, or a mountain scene. See it with as much detail as you desire. Do this for one to five minutes without a break; repeat throughout the day for a relaxing break.

- *Switching your focus* will improve your eye's ability to change focus clearly from near to far distances and back, which is perhaps the most frequently performed function of the eye. Set your sight on a calendar or wall clock far enough away so that the numbers or letters on it are just readable. Then hold a book or memo near your eyes, but far enough away so that you can focus on it. Read three numbers or letters far away, then immediately read three nearby. Do this several times until it is comfortable. Now move the book or memo several inches closer, and repeat the exercise. Do this several times a day for one minute.
- *Eye rolling* is an exercise that relieves tension. Without moving your head, glance around to the extreme corners of the room slowly and rhythmically. Close your eyes for ten seconds, and repeat in the opposite direction. Now roll your eyes in large circles for thirty seconds, then reverse. Finally, fixate on a spot on a distant wall; keeping your eyes on it, roll your head around first one way, then the other.

Get Aerobic Exercise

Aerobic exercise increases the amount of oxygen your blood carries, thus feeding a rich supply to the retina. Rods and cones immediately begin degenerating with impaired blood supply.

People who get little exercise have less oxygen in their blood, which limits the potential of their eyesight. Exercise also reduces overall stress that affects vision.

Eat a Balanced Diet

Rods and cones suffer from loss of nutrition. Foods from all four of the food groups provide the vitamins, minerals, and protein upon which the eye depends. These vital substances include Vitamin A (essential for the rods to work, and thus associated with night vision), the B vitamins (for converting glucose, a form of sugar, into energy. The retina ranks second only to the brain in the rate at which it breaks down glucose to properly function), and Vitamin C (Vitamin C takes up one-third of the eye's weight, and the eye has twenty times the amount of Vitamin C in its fluids than any other body fluid). Vitamin C may help prevent cataracts and relieve glaucoma. Additionally, Vitamins D and E, iron, copper, zinc, calcium, and protein all play significant roles in eye health.

Have Regular Eye Exams

Eye doctors check not only for visual acuity, but also for diseases that can diminish or obliterate sight. The most common are cataracts, a gradually clouding of the cornea, and glaucoma, increasing pressure inside the eye that can lead to blindness.

Protect Eyes From Glare and Injury

Ultraviolet light can burn your retina (reflection of sun off snow causes "snow blindness") and may promote cataracts. Wear good sunglasses and shade your eyes with a hat. You will enjoy viewing the day more from open, shaded eyes, than from squinted, unprotected eyes. The Eskimos fashioned sunglasses from thin disks of bone with a slit in the center; that way they could scan with wide open eyes yet not suffer the effects of sunlight and glare. Ultraviolet light poses great danger in our urban world, where buildings, cars, and smooth roads reflect enormous amounts of light.

Don't Smoke

Smoking destroys Vitamin B_{12}, which is necessary to maintain an insulating coat of myelin around the optic nerve. Vision dims when this coating degenerates. The damage usually reverses when smoking ceases.

Look Into the Distance

Relieve your eyes often by looking at a distant scene, especially if you spend a lot of time reading, working at a computer, or doing other near-point tasks.

— Fun with Vision —

Our complex vision gives us many avenues of exploration. In addition to the double vision and blind spot tests earlier in this chapter, use the following activities to enjoy playing with vision.

See a "Star"

Look to the right, then press your finger against your upper left eyelid at the outer corner where your lids meet. See the flash of light in the direction you're looking. Because the retina is only equipped for light sensation, any pressure applied to it registers as light stimulation. This is why you see "stars" after being hit in the eye or head.

The Dominant Eye

One of your eyes takes charge as the "main" eye. To discover this, make a circle with the thumb and forefinger of one hand, and hold it at arms length. Line up any small, distant target in the circle. Now close your left eye. If the target is still in the circle, you used your right eye to align it, and the right eye dominates. Now close your right eye. If the target was in the circle before, it will now disappear, since you did not use the left eye to align it. If the opposite happens, the target disappearing when you close your left eye and reappearing in the circle when you close your right, your left eye dominates. Now look in a mirror; the dominant eye is usually the larger of the two.

Hole in the Hand

Roll a sheet of paper lengthwise to make an eleven-inch tube. Put the tube up to one eye, and focus on an object. Now put your other hand a few inches in front of your free eye, palm toward you and side of the hand touching the tube. Now open both eyes; you will see the object through a hole in your hand! This graphically shows how the brain puts together the two views from each eye to create one view. (Side note: you probably put the tube up to your dominant eye.)

Speed Read

Without any effort, you will instantly read 25 percent faster by simply covering the material you have already read with a blank card or piece of paper. Move the card down the page as you read, always keeping it just above wherever your eyes are. This simple act reduces the constant random saccades, or unconscious scans of the eye. Even though you think you are keeping your eye on the line of type and moving it steadily along, it is really flicking all around, taking in a line in about eleven jumps (remember, it can only clearly see what appears on the fovea), and jerking back to material you've already read. Covering the previous type eliminates much of the stimuli that attracts the eye, and the eye stays more on task. Saccades will still occur when you cover the previous lines, but they will direct to material not yet read, which speeds your reading.

Retina Road Map

Many blood vessels feed the retina, and when light travels past them they cast shadows on your retina. Your brain fills in vision over these shadows, since they are in the same place all the time. To see their branching pattern, darken the room and move a flashlight around near the side of your eye.

In bright daylight you may notice dark specks floating past your field of vision. These are also shadows, the remnants of additional blood vessels that dissolved in the last three months of your fetal life.

Tilt Your World

This activity can lift your spirits and even make you laugh out loud, partly because it makes you dizzy and partly because it is fun to view the world from a different perspective. Tilt your head all the way to one side, so that the world looks sideways. Now walk down a hallway, open drawers, pick up objects — just experience the world with different vision for a few minutes.

The Painter's View

When I was young, my mother led me through an exercise that forever opened my visual mind. We were sitting at the dinner table, and she asked, "What color is that birch tree outside?" I told her it was white, and thought her question rather obvious. "Is it really?" she asked, and I looked again. As I searched its silky bark, it dawned on me that it was not white at all. The setting sun made the western edge of the bark buttery yellow, and brown slits decorated that side. The yellow merged into a light gray facing toward me, the slits now jet black. As I followed the colors to the eastern side, the bark was an electric blue, with navy-black slits. In fact, when I really looked at it, there was no white to be found.

Look at a tree, and identify all the colors you see. Look at the different colors of your car, depending upon the light and shadow. Your houseplant's leaves, previously thought of as "green," may really be patterns of cream, yellow, brown, gray, lime green, forest green, blue-green. Notice the variations in a black dog's coat; it may shine white, or appear navy blue where certain shadows fall. Up close you may even see the spectrum in the hairs as the sun hits them.

Visual Complements

Your color vision has pairs of "opposites"—red/green and yellow/blue. When you saturate your vision with one of these colors, the opposite will appear in an after-effect. For example, when a camera flashes its yellow light in your eyes, you see a blue dot dancing in your vision afterward. Find a bright red sheet of paper, and stare at it for a full minute. Then close your eyes, and you will see a green rectangle.

Vision floods us with the beauty of light, color, line, shadow, and shape. Care for this delicate sense so that you may retain the pleasure of seeing a loved one's face, a thundercloud, a movie, a river valley. Enjoy marveling in your body's windows, the eyes.

6

The Unacknowledged Senses

Throughout history philosophers and scientists have categorized as many as seventeen senses. People have simply settled on the classical five senses of the previous chapters as arbitrary categorizations. But as complex, highly evolved beings, we have many more than five senses. Some of those senses will be explored here; however, surely more are to be discovered as humans continually probe deeper into the complexities of mind and matter.

— Balance —

The continual, split-second adjustments of weight and muscle as you walk are only possible because you have a well-developed sense of balance. Anyone who

walks on two legs has it. Bicyclists have it. Gymnasts doing flips and cartwheels on four-inch balance beams have it. A cat walking on a thin branch has it. Monkeys leaping from tree to tree have it. We enjoy challenging its boundaries in dance and sports, and seek to confuse it for pleasure.

Your inner ear houses three looping tubes called the semicircular canals, each oriented differently to sense horizontal, vertical, and diagonal movement. Fluid inside these tubes bends tiny bristle hairs depending upon how your head moves. The hairs send electrochemical nerve impulses to the brain via the vestibular nerve to inform the brain of position or balance changes. The brain then fires signals to the appropriate muscles to maintain equilibrium. This system is so well-developed that you easily keep your balance in complete darkness, and know your position underwater.

While people can maintain balance even without using sight, vision is an important component to the complete balance system, as is the proprioreceptive sense of muscles and joints with their sense of position. When vision and the inner ear sense conflicting things, it is hard to resolve the difference.

Experimenters have created rooms that can be tilted. A subject is seated in the normally-aligned room, in a chair that can be independently adjusted. The room and all its contents are then tilted, and the subject has to adjust the chair until she believes she is upright according to the outside world. Some people do align the chair based on their inner ear sense, which results in correct balance, and some use vision, which results in their align-

ing the chair with the room and being tilted in comparison to the outside world.

Balance is the chief function of the ear in many creatures, and seems to be the reason ears first developed. Primeval fish needed organs to keep them balanced in their ocean home. These organs were originally fluid-filled sacs lined with receptor cells. When the fish moved, the sacs converted the fluid motion into neural impulses to inform the creature if it was on an even keel, swimming upward, downward, or in circles. This functioning resembles that of our own semi-circular canals. Eventually the organ developed into the swim or air bladder we find in most bony fishes.

I enjoy swinging for the rush of exhilarating confusion I feel as I swoop forward and up, backward and down, backward and up, forward and down. When we disturb our sense of relationship to space so that our brains can't make the necessary changes fast enough to maintain the sense of balance, we experience the giddiness of swinging, or the dizziness of twirling in a swivel chair. Dizziness can feel wonderful; children twirl each other and roll down hills, dancers swing each other. A religious sect uses spinnning and twirling to help reach a point of spiritual ecstasy. A more pronounced dizziness, termed vertigo, affects some people so that their surroundings seem to spin for no apparent reason.

People's capacity to adjust to new motions varies considerably. Some people abhor rides at the state fair while others seek them out for the light-headed thrill; some people get car- and sea-sick more easily than others.

— Balancing Fun —

Test your sense of balance with the following exercises.

Take a Spin

Put the book down and stand up. Close your eyes, then spin around in place four times quickly. Open your eyes and feel the slow, thick feeling in your head as you reorient yourself, and watch the world go from flurried motion to a standstill. Enjoy the feeling of gradually regaining equilibrium.

State Patrol's Secret

Since alcohol impairs the delicate sense of balance, police officers often use this quick test to see if someone has been drinking. Stand up, arms relaxed at your sides. Lift one foot off the ground and balance for fifteen seconds on the other foot. Notice the lightning-fast adjustments your foot, ankle, knee, leg, torso, arms, shoulders, and head make as you strive to maintain balance. Now, close your eyes and do the same thing—you'll find it much more difficult to balance when you subtract visual cues from the inner ear sense. Appreciate the intricate interactions of all the large and tiny muscles.

The Necessary Center

Stand sideways with your right foot against the baseboard of a wall, your feet ten inches apart. Try to lift your left foot: you won't be able to! To balance, you must be able to shift your body's weight to a central line where there is equal weight on each side of center. The wall to your right prevents you from shifting your center of gravity to the right, which is essential to lifting your left foot. This unconscious adjusting of the center of gravity allows you to rise from chairs, pick up objects, and carry things without toppling over.

The Log Roll

Find a grassy hill. Lie down at the top and roll to the bottom like a log. Enjoy gravity's pull and the confusion you'll feel at the bottom. You may end up laughing from pure pleasure! You can experience a mini version of this by lying on a flat, soft surface (carpet or grass) and rolling sideways.

— Solar Sense —

In the middle of your forehead, you have another eye. In humans it is buried beneath the skull; in reptiles, amphibians, and birds it is just under the skin. This is the pea-sized pineal gland, an essential photosensor that synchronizes animal (and human) actions to day length. Lizards sense light directly through the gland; in humans it appears to be stimulated by the light coming in through

our eyes. The pineal gland is the key photoreceptor of an independent sensory system that is not part of vision or any sense.

The lonely little pineal ranks as the only organ in the brain that is not bilateral. One of evolution's oldest organs, it may be left over from a time before bilateral symmetry developed. Descartes claimed it was the seat of the human soul. Eastern religions consider the "third eye" to be the means through which the inner self sees divine revelation. In a yoga exercise, people close their eyes and have someone hold an index finger half an inch away from the middle of their forehead; many people see a bright area of light, indicating that the pineal has been stimulated.

The pineal primarily serves as a synchronizing clock to keep animals and humans internally aligned with the gradually changing day length as the year progresses. In humans and other diurnal animals, darkness causes the pineal to release melatonin, a hormone that inhibits activity and sexual functioning (and probably causes us to grow drowsy as night falls). Conversely, as morning dawns, the pineal stops secreting melatonin and activity and sexual levels rise. Many people intensely enjoy sexual activity in the morning because they are not working against the effects of melatonin.

This gland serves to keep our natural body rhythms in sync with the day and the year. People who experimentally lived in caves entirely devoid of sunlight kept a regular waking and sleeping cycle, but their days gradually stretched to around twenty-six hours instead of twenty-four. The pineal gland keeps circadian (Latin for "about a day") rhythms roped in to match the sun's cycle.

Animals also have circannual rhythms that are fine-tuned to nature by action of the pineal gland. As the autumn days shorten,

the pineal releases more melatonin, causing each creature to make the changes necessary to prepare for winter, whether it be changing fur from brown to white like the snowshoe hare, growing a thicker coat like the wolf, decreasing appetite demands like deer, sheep, and goats, or seeking a den for a long winter's hibernation like the bear. Humans, too, respond to the waning light with decreased sex drive.

As the days grow longer and signal spring, the pineal gland decreases production of melatonin and spurs birds to migrate (their sex hormones increase, a major trigger of migration). Humans' thoughts turn to dalliance and romance in a phenomenon we call "spring fever." Our sexual hormones increase along with the increased light.

Experiments have proven the importance of this solar sense. Humans' biological "day" lengthens without the cues of the sun. However, a bee's day shortens, as shown in experiments under unchanging light and temperature. Bees also use the position of the sun as a marker in the elaborate dance they do to tell other bees about a source of food. As the day goes on, the dance changes to accommodate the changing position of the sun.

Lizards rely on the pineal gland to cue them when to bask in the sun and when to seek shade, as well as how to find home. They lack good vision, and the angle of the sun on the pineal indicates the direction of home. When experimenters have covered the pineal with reflective foil, the reptiles spend more time basking, are less able to find their way home, and show marked changes in the breeding cycle, as if reproductive activity had been put on fast forward.

Even plants have this solar sense. Changing seasonal light causes them to lose leaves in the fall and run sap in the spring, while daily light changes trigger opening and closing of flowers. We notice a disturbance in our own process of adjusting from light to dark when we rapidly cross time zones in a transoceanic flight. We can quickly reset our watch, but our body clock takes many days to adjust. The pineal produces the inhibiting melatonin just when we want to be active, causing jet lag.

In our increasingly artificial environment, few of us get regular, meaningful exposure to the rhythm of the sun and seasons. "Winter depression" often affects urban dwellers, who become lethargic and dull during the day and unable to sleep at night. Locked as they are in an artificial environment, they do not get sufficient natural light for their master clock to synchronise with that of the sun, and their "day" grows longer. The remedy for this is exposure to intense bright light at certain times of day to reset their body clocks.

— Getting Your Fill —

Expose yourself to the natural rhythms of natural light. Here are a few exercises to help you overcome the effects of artificial environments.

Get Outside

If you have an indoor job, get outside at lunch, in the morning, or during an afternoon break, to stay connected with the natural

day. (Always wear sunscreen and sunglasses; you'll still receive the healthy benefits of natural light with less of the damage from ultraviolet rays). Adopt more outdoor activities, even if it's simply reading outdoors. The sun stimulates production of Vitamin D in your body and keeps your internal "day" in line with the world.

Let Natural Light Guide You

Occasionally allow your schedule to be guided by the natural light. Several times a year for a week at a time, I abandon watches and clocks and sleep under the stars (or in a tent if the weather demands). The dawn rays awaken me, the blue transparent night puts me to bed, and I feel a peaceful connectedness with the world and my body as they are supposed to be.

Enjoy the Moonlight

Stay in touch with the moon, especially if you are female. While this sounds suspiciously fanciful, there are sound natural reasons for being exposed to moonlight. The female menstrual cycle averages one lunar rhythm, 29.5 days. The average human gestation period is exactly nine lunar cycles.

The moon exerts a pull on the Earth four times stronger than the sun (due to distance), and causes the great oceans of the world to bulge toward it as it circles Earth. How arrogant of us to think that a force that causes tides has no affect on us, who are composed of 95 percent water!

I worked in a customer service department where we began charting irate calls when we realized they surged at certain times of the moon. While we know the moon affects humans, it's not clear whether it's the gravitational pull or the light itself (or both). In the modern industrial world, few people get enough exposure to moonlight to be able to synchronise with it. However, experiments have shown that exposing women to artificial moonlight for only three consecutive nights, once a month, caused their cycles to coincide with the lunar rhythm.

An accepted fertility technique to help standardize irregular menstrual cycles is to keep the sleeping room dark during the dark of the moon, and leave a low light on during the full moon. The body (probably the pineal gland) interprets this as moonlight. The more predictable menstrual cycles that result help couples plan conception.

When I moved to a city apartment, twenty-five floors high, I feared I would feel too disconnected from nature. I found, however, that my menstrual cycle quickly changed to begin with each full moon. The large southern-facing windows next to my bed gave me a larger dose of night light than I had ever had in less urban settings. Similarly, on an extended trip to New Zealand, I started out with an eighteen-day cycle until it settled into the lunar rhythm of my new location. Female expedition members find that their menstrual cycles synchronize with the moon whenever they spend extended periods of time living and sleeping outdoors.

— Magnetic Sense —

The mystery of how birds migrate great distances with absolute accuracy puzzled humans for centuries. Only recently have we discovered a previously unknown sense, the homing or magnetic sense. Birds rely heavily on visual cues like landmarks and the sun and stars for navigation, to be sure. They may also use their memory of scents as navigational markings. But when these cues are not present, such as when cloud cover prevents birds from seeing the ground or stars, they rely on their magnetic sense.

Earth is one big magnet, oriented north to south. We are discovering more and more that animals, and maybe humans, are sensitive to its magnetic lines, which curve and vary like a topographic map due to differences in underlying rocks. It is thought that young birds develop a celestial compass using their magnetic sense to orient themselves to the sun and stars. Throughout their lifetimes, they fall back on this magnetic sense when visibility is poor, feeling the angle of the invisible magnetic lines against their bodies as they fly through them. Whales navigate along this magnetic map, using the lines like roads. Sometimes they follow a path so intently that a whole group will strand themselves on the beach. Examination of stranding sites has shown that they occur where the magnetic lines ran directly from sea to shore. Bees orient their honeycombs with a certain east to west angle, and will change it upon application of an artificial magnetic field.

These animals and insects contain magnetite, an iron compound, in their bodies. It is thought that even a minute amount of this mineral will provide sensitivity to Earth's magnetic field. Magnetite has been found in the stomachs of bees, between the

brain and skull of dolphins, in the skull bones of migratory fish such as yellowfin tuna and chinook salmon, and in the brains of certain bird species. Recent studies are discovering magnetite in the human brain as well. The greatest amount of magnetite has been found in monarch butterflies, who perform the longest migration in the insect world, some 2,500 miles.

Experiments on birds have shown that the magnetic sense takes over when the sun is not available. In one study, an electromagnet was placed on a homing pigeon's head to distort the magnetic environment. When the bird was allowed to see the sun, it oriented itself correctly toward home, despite the polarity of the electromagnet. However, when the sun was hidden, the magnetic sense took over and the bird misoriented itself, following the pull of the electromagnet.

There is some evidence that humans, too, have a magnetic sense. In tests at Manchester University in England, groups of students were blindfolded and taken on a coachride. Half the subjects had strong magnets on their heads, and half wore non-magnetic metal bars. When the coach stopped and the students were asked to point toward home, those without the magnetic bars performed significantly better than those with the magnets. Other tests have proven similar results, while studies elsewhere have not supported these findings.

While it is not yet conclusive that humans have a homing sense, I find that some people are very good at sensing direction, even when visual clues such as sun and star positions are unavailable. I was once teamed with an experienced nature photographer and hunter on a bear research project in which we used radar to track a collared black bear on its daily activities in the woods. The

bear meandered through swamps, dense thickets, along rock ridges, and deep into hollows, following its own well-developed spatial sense and thoroughly confounding our sense of direction. At dusk, when the bear had bedded down, we were to make our way back to the research station. We happened upon an old road and were able to assess our bearings. The overcast sky gave no clue to direction, and we weren't even sure what direction would be correct anyway. I had a strong sense, however, that the research lab was in a certain direction, though I could not say how I knew this. The experienced hunter was guessing a different direction, and I acquiesced in deference to his many years of experience in the field. We started in that direction, against my very strong feeling, until the honk of the research lab truck tracked us down. We were walking in the wrong direction. When in doubt, and there isn't a clue such as a western setting sun, moss-covered north side of trees, or north star, tune in to your possible homing sense.

Dowsing, the ability to locate underground water, is thought to be another manifestation of our magnetic sense. Dowsers walk along holding a divining rod, usually a forked stick, in front of them. The rod suddenly dips to indicate water lying just below ground. The uncanny accuracy of dowsers may be due to their sensitivity to magnetic fluctuations in the Earth's surface. A body of underground water would cause a significant change in the magnetic pattern, and their arm muscles, minutely fatigued from holding the rod, twitch in response to the difference.

— ESP —

You get a strong feeling that you should call your friend in another state. The feeling persists, and you call, only to find out that she had just been rushed to the hospital as a result of a car crash. Did you experience telepathy, a communication between minds through means other than the ordinary senses? Or coincidence, since it had been awhile since you talked and it was natural to want to call about that time?

You predict that the newspaper headlines one week from today will include news that the House passed a health care bill by 150 votes, a teenager suffered gunshot wounds, and a bank was robbed. The newspaper comes out and includes headlines almost exactly like these. Is it precognition, knowledge of the future? Or educated, likely guesses based upon what you know about that newspaper, the area, and current events?

A couple comes to dinner for the first time at your house, and say they brought you a gift which is out in the car. You know it is a large bottle of red California wine—and it is. Could it be clairvoyance, a knowledge of a person, object, or event acquired without the use of normal senses? Or is it an unconscious process of elimination you've gone through to determine the likely gift based on the situation and what you know about these people?

Extra-sensory perception, or ESP, is an inclusive term for telepathy, precognition, and clairvoyance, as well as other phenomena such as astral travel, past lives regression, and psychokinesis (ability to move objects or influence events through mental, not physical, power). All of us have experienced ESP-like things: déjà vu, a feeling of having been somewhere before even though

you know you haven't been; dreams that come true; knowing what someone was going to say before he or she said it; feeling you are being stared at and turning around to find it's true; or "willing" someone to turn around, and he or she does.

While many educated and scientific people agree that "paranormal" events do occur, controversy haunts the explanations. Despite extensive laboratory testing with cards and dice, repeatable, reliable, scientific proof of ESP eludes us.

A common theory of ESP says it is energy detected by a separate, "sixth" sense that we have yet to uncover. Others, including me, attribute it to sensory signals transmitted and received by the body that are below the normal threshold of a known sensory system.

Researchers at New York University have measured extermely fine electrical activity in the brain from just above the scalp, and have found that the shifts in brain activity resulting from different types of thought can be recorded from outside the body. This discovery suggests that the activity of the brain may actually project out beyond the scalp. As you have read, human senses are already designed to pick up parts of the electromagnetic spectrum; perhaps we'll find that some people's thresholds are lower than normal and they can actually sense others' brain waves.

Humans can go beyond what we currently understand as the limits of our five senses. We know that colors affect mood; this seemingly paranormal effect may be a sensitivity to an area of the electromagnetic spectrum which is outside the normally defined range we can see. Remember how a mother could identify a T-shirt her child had worn from several other identical shirts? Before the discovery of pheromones, this would have appeared

paranormal. It is then a short jump to believe that someone we think is "psychic" has a highly developed sense of smell and could sense another's emotional state through pheromones, which we already know change in response to emotion.

We are quick to reject anything that seems to defy the laws of nature, forgetting that our understanding of the world is woefully limited and often incorrect. The Hungarian obstetrician Ignaz Semmelweis first theorized that unseen substances caused the 20 percent mortality rate of women who gave birth, and began the practice of washing his hands and instruments with antiseptic before assisting delivery.

Though bacteria was yet unknown, he had hit upon the solution to the death rate, and the mortality of his patients dropped to a record low. Unfortunately, the medical establishment of Europe rejected his views and continued killing thousands by practicing medicine with unwashed hands. The medical community insulted and criticized Semmelweis so thoroughly for suggesting that unseen substances caused disease and illness that he went insane under the pressure and died at age forty-eight. Sickness and death were attributed to paranormal causes such as the ill will of the gods until humans invented instruments powerful enough to see microbes.

Just as the discovery of germs forever changed the face of medicine, modern physics has rocked our definitions of time, space, energy, and matter. For example, our concept of substance has entirely changed. Our former view of atoms as the smallest physical units of matter is now altered with the discovery of even more elementary particles—particles that don't even exist as solid matter. So, too, has changed our narrow definition of time

as a linear flow. The idea of past, present, and future has given way to a quantum physics understanding of time as symmetrical, flowing both forward and backward simultaneously. Positrons are electrons flowing backward, anti-matter is matter moving in a negative-time direction.

Absolute space and time were simply our limited definition of a far more complex universe. We now know of black holes in space so dense even light cannot escape, and find that sympathetic action between formerly-joined elementary particles can occur instantly regardless of the distance separating them.

Science is embracing "chaos," the interconnectedness of all things. A butterfly fanning its wings in the Amazon rainforest has impact on the rest of the world as if everything shares a huge, universal web. We are proving the idea of fundamental unity as expressed by Hippocrates: "There is one common flow, one common breathing, all things are in sympathy." The concept was basic to Native Americans and other indigenous peoples and was held around the world until the eighteenth century brought its mechanistic view that still permeates common thought today.

The seemingly fantastic propositions of ESP appear almost unremarkable compared to these truly astounding discoveries. I have no trouble believing that our senses can pick up signals so subtle we are not aware of them, and that our unconscious can quietly or suddenly present them to us.

For example, we have photographed the human aura, an energy field surrounding us that changes its nature and size with varying states of our being. Perhaps someone with touch sensitivity beyond what we consider the norm can feel this aura. Some people are able to see this aura.

The great mentalist Kreskin believes that his unsurpassed powers of reading people's thoughts, finding lost objects, and predicting events are sensed through the same five senses we all have. He calls ESP "extra-sensitive perception" and believes it may be nothing more than extremely sensitive development of the ordinary senses on an unconscious level. He has spent a lifetime purposely developing his senses, and believes they constantly pick up information he doesn't consciously notice. He uses deep relaxation and concentration to increase access to all the information.

Develop Your "Extra-Sensitive Perception"

The following tips can help you to more fully develop your "extra-sensitive perception."

- Use exercises in this book to fine tune each of your senses, gradually stretching them to higher sensitivity.
- Deeply relax at least once a day to "turn off" the conscious mind and release bodily tension. Lie down, and starting with your facial muscles, tighten and relax each muscle of your body until you have reached the toes. Fill your mind with a soothing color such as light blue, light green, light gray, or beige.
- Follow hunches. Pay attention to those thoughts that are atypical of you or seem to come out of nowhere. If you are afraid of flying and get a "feeling" that your plane is going to crash, it is

probably fear rather than intuitive information. But when you have a feeling that is unusual for you, pay extra attention.

- Consider extra-sensitive perception a natural and integral part of your being; a birthright.

— Trigeminal Sense —

We have a penchant for oral gratification outside of taste and odor. A specialized network of nerves in our faces and heads carry information about touch and temperature sensations. The touch sensations of smoking, nail-biting, teeth-picking, and moustache-licking please us immensely. We grow almost addicted to sensations that feel like temperature but are actually separate from it; the "heat" or "cold" rises through the roofs of our mouths, shoots through our noses and spreads into our foreheads. Think of the "burning" sensation of carbonated beverages, Chinese mustard, or hot chili peppers. Remember the cool spreading of menthol cough drops. All this sensation relies on the trigeminal system.

— Synesthesia —

At birth, humans appear to be synesthetic, meaning boundaries between the senses do not exist. One sensory experience will trigger perception by another system. Blind babies will turn eyes toward a sound; even sighted babies will reach out for a sound in a dark room. It may be that infants see sounds as easily as they hear them. As a child matures, the brain becomes more specialized,

and the boundaries between the senses will be erected. By age six months a child actually senses less than at birth. Some adults experience synesthesia, and are able to see sounds, or hear smells. Speech often elicits colors for the synesthete, with higher, more compressed vowel sounds evoking white, yellow, and the brighter colors, while long vowels stimulate brown, black, and more somber colors. The person may see a small object and simultaneously hear a high-pitched, squeaky sound; a deeper, fuller sound will accompany large objects. Several times when talking quickly I have made verbal errors such as "I caught a whiff of myself in the mirror" or "When she glimpsed the flavor, she smiled," and each time I think of the people for whom those phrases might be literal!

— Electrical Sense —

Many of us know someone who can predict rain by a pain in the elbow. Before a storm, the air becomes charged with positive ions, which are known to influence the amount of the hormone serotonin in mammals. Serotonin controls sleep and other metabolic processes, and helps alleviate pain. This "weather sense" could account for the depression or aches and pains some people feel before a storm. Bees sense electrical fields, and before a thunderstorm become agitated and return to the hive in droves. Furry animals, with much drier skin than humans, conduct electricity very well and become literally electrified before a storm or earthquake (they register the electromagnetic changes in the earth prior to the quake we recognize). They become physically uncom-

fortable and exhibit erratic and unusual behavior before these natural events. Cats may suddenly leave the house, horses stampede, or dogs howl.

— Proprioreceptive (Kinesthetic) Sense —

Muscles, joints, ligaments, and tendons sport receptors that respond to movement. Every time you move they tell the brain what's going on — for example, that there is a pitching boat deck underfoot, or that you're shaking your foot. They provide a deep sense of position that sends a neural picture to your brain.

Try this: Close your eyes and stretch your arms out to your sides, hands open and fingers apart. Now bring your hands together a few inches in front of your chest, until your fingertips meet exactly with the other hand. Try it until you can do it perfectly; you are relying solely on the proprioreceptive sense. Vary the challenge by touching the tip of your earlobes with the index finger.

This chapter mentions only a few of our less-recognized senses. Thinking we have only five senses is as outdated as thinking the earth is flat. As we explore further both the grandeur of the universe and the very stuff that composes life and matter, we will surely uncover more of our amazing senses.

7

Symphony of
the Senses

Hot rocks glow red in the center of a dark sweat
lodge. Twelve people sit or kneel in a circle around
the low rock pit, feeling dry heat emanate from the
stones. Sparks spatter and spit where sprinkled cedar
leaves dance on the rocks, the sweet scent filling the
low, dome-shaped lodge. The drummer taps a rapid
rhythm on a stretched skin drum, the high sound
alive in close quarters, and singers raise their voices
in traditional song.

At a certain point, the leader ladles water onto
the rocks. The hissing of a thousand snakes accompanies a hot, curling plume of sage- and cedar-scented
steam. It fills lungs, burns faces, permeates muscle.
Participants give themselves over to intense,
extended rounds of songs, prayers, drumming, and

more steam. At the conclusion of the ceremony, the leader throws open the door. Outdoor light and air flood the lodge, providing tingling relief for hot, wet skin. Bodies steam and smoke as if on fire. People drink in scents of grass and forest, and pass a ladle to relish a drink of cool, sweet water. One by one they leave the lodge to find a quiet place to sit and savor immense peace. When ready, they return for a feast to replenish themselves.

This Native American purification ceremony combines the senses to link people with the divine much as an orchestra combines many instruments to create a piece of profound beauty. We can score our own symphony daily through a combined awareness and use of our senses. So integral are our senses to life that enhanced sensuality leads us to experience each moment of daily life as a gift.

The Japanese tea ceremony elevates to an art form the making and sharing of a bowl of tea. It venerates every element; each sound, smell, movement, and feeling in what could otherwise be thought of as a "throw-away" or mundane task. The ceremony takes place in a quiet place, where guests first admire seasonal flowers displayed in a simple, understated way. With great tranquility the server kneels on a straw mat and uses precise, ballet-like movements to spoon the tea into a bowl, ladle hot water into it, froth it with a bamboo whisk, and hand it to the first guest with a bow. Guests bow, slowly turn the warm bowl in a prescribed way, drink the tea, and admire the tea bowl. Respect for the utensils used in the ceremony extends even to the cleaning of them before and after as the guests watch.

— Seeking Sensual Experience —

We value life more by intentionally appreciating the most of each moment. I happened to be in Jacksonville, Florida, and had driven out to the beach to walk and pick shells during the last light of day. When darkness and high tide sent me back to my car, there were forty to fifty people sitting in lawn chairs or on blankets, looking east out to sea. Figuring there must be a fireworks display in the offing, I sat down to watch as well.

Then it dawned on me that the newspaper had said the full moon about to occur would be 4,000 miles closer than usual, an orbit that occurs less than once per century. To my wonder and delight, all these people had gathered to watch the rise of the full moon! Forsaking television and their other usual activities, they were intentionally out to savor a beautiful sight. The moon did rise, full and yellow and bigger than anyone had ever seen it. Spectators oohed and aahed, took videotapes of it, admired its wide silvery path glimmering on the ocean, moved closer together in their blankets, and gazed at the orb until high clouds obscured it.

Occasionally seek sensual immersion from experts, then weave what you learn into daily life. Experience a professional massage; eat at a restaurant where a chef values how food looks as well as tastes; go hear live music. At a spa in Wisconsin, sensuality reaches its height. Lush wooded grounds along the wild St. Croix River set the mood of abiding peace and relaxation. Inside the 1908 mansion, quiet music wafts through air barely scented with plant and flower essences. Guests experience massage with fragrant essential oils, hot body wraps of soft, natural materials, organic food elegantly presented, and full-body "polishing" with

seven pulsing shower heads massaging energy points along the spine. Bedrooms gleam spare and elegant, with bare wood floors, white walls, dark antique headboards and beige sheets of unbleached, undyed cotton. Aromatherapists prescribe scents to entice the effects one desires, or allow one to instinctively choose. A person comes away with a calm mind and revived senses, and with the reminder that most sensual pleasures are readily available—a green herb garnishing your dinner; a dab of scented oil to coax you into a nap; a hot bath; a walk in the woods.

Embracing the Unexpected

Sensuous living means seeking out such sensual experiences, as well as taking sensual opportunities that present themselves unbidden. I just came in from an unexpected drenching while in-line skating at a local park reserve. Initially I was piqued that rain foiled my one chance for good exercise that day. So, rather than stop my activity when the wind picked up and smelled like rain, I decided to keep skating and see what would happen.

My attitude quickly migrated from irritation to intense interest; I felt all my senses liven because I was doing something unexpected and unfamiliar. I began enjoying first the cold pin-pricks of a sprinkle, then the pelting of a full-fledged downpour. My wheels hissed as they spun and spat a stream of water in front of me. My clothes suctioned to me like a clammy second skin. Rivulets raced into my eyes and mouth and sectioned my hair into melted icicles. I began laughing at how ridiculous it was—and how exhilarating.

When water pooled too deep on the tar for safe blading, I headed for the car. But the blue-gray sky, warm rain, and beckoning forest were truly too wonderful to leave. I took off my skates, peeled off my sopping socks, and ran into the rain again, barefoot. The earth and all its sharp things were softened enough that I could pad along trails painlessly. I squeezed brownie-doughlike mud between my toes. Splashed through puddles. Swirled hands and feet in the Mississippi, wading thigh deep since I couldn't get any wetter than I already was.

A turtle ducked its head; a great blue heron lifted out of the rushes and croaked its way across the river, wingspan as wide as I am tall. Two Canadian geese necked and preened mid-stream. I scrambled up the riverbank and sniffed every blossom and flower, from electric-blue violets hugging the ground to pink crabapple blossoms. Standing stock-still, I watched a brilliant goldfinch flit and twitch nearby. Thunder rumbled in the distant background, and rain whispered in the grass and leaves around me. I threw rocks into the river to hear their indignant plunk, and fingered nascent leaves just popped from their casings. Skidding down muddy slopes like a clumsy skier, dancing over pebbles, gingerly peering at a large dead fish, I thoroughly enjoyed myself.

— Integrating the Senses —

Here are some activities to help you integrate all your senses, to enjoy all the pleasures sitting outside your door. I hope these are seed for many more.

Relish an Orange

You could perfunctorily cut an orange in quarters, eat it in thirty seconds flat, notice the taste briefly, and be on with your busy day. At least once in awhile, try a more sensual way. Grasp an orange in both palms, feeling the round fullness and its smooth, pocked peel. Toss it into the air and catch it, appreciating the way it grows smaller as it goes farther away, larger as it comes back. Enjoy the weight and mass as it hits your hands again.

Now bite the skin so that you have a place to start peeling. Taste the acid spurt of oil from the peel. Begin peeling the orange, listening to the light tearing sound. Watch the spray as you bend the peel back, and smell its citric pungency in the air. Once peeled, examine the orange with its translucent inner skin that mutes the inside color and divides neat sections. Nutritious white shreds from the inside of the peel mottle the globe as clouds cloak the earth.

Push your thumbs into one plump end and pull the orange in two, admiring the slight sucking sound of sections splitting. Break one section in half to reveal the brilliant color inside, and rotate it slightly to watch light glisten on the juicy fruit. Mouth one unbroken section and marvel at how there is almost no taste; then bite to puncture it and feel the flood of cool juice and brilliant, sweet taste.

The Sensual Letter

At night, write a letter to someone you care about, whether he or she lives across the ocean or across the room. If it is a warm season, sit naked by a breezy window; if chilly, wrap yourself in a soft robe or sweatsuit, without underwear, bra, or other impediments. Light a candle at the table, or several, until you have enough light for writing (remember that your eyes take a long time to adjust to dim light; what may appear too dark at first becomes plenty once you've adjusted).

Hand write this letter—a computer or typewriter breaks the seamless, sensual flow. Put on relaxing, instrumental music, at low volume. Make a cup of fragrant herbal tea and let its steam scent your writing area. Let yourself relax, and begin.

If you don't know what to say, start by describing your setting and its sensations. "I'm sitting nude at my table right now, with three candles flickering as my only light. My lemon tea smells sweet and I'm listening to a peaceful tape of piano music. The breeze feels good on my skin, and I thought of you..." You may end up being a more frequent correspondent if you make the act something beautiful to look forward to.

Wine-tasting

Enophiles use all their senses to experience wine. You can follow their example. Choose a beverage made of natural elements, such as wine or juice. Soft drinks, artificial fruit drinks, and other "synthetic" beverages do not have rich qualities that are rewarding to savor.

Begin by pouring your wine into a glass goblet. The liquid should not be too cold, as coldness inhibits aroma and chills taste buds. Eliminate distraction, so you can direct all your attention to each step. This way your sensory thresholds will be lower. Look at the wine, holding it up to the light to view its rich color. Notice its clarity; watch as you swirl the glass and it leaves "fingers" on the sides. Swirling increases the aroma and bouquet, which you smell as you now pass the glass back and forth under your nose. The aroma arises from the type of grape used in making the wine. Bouquet develops from fermentation, processing, or aging.

Now you are ready to taste it. Take a small sip, and roll it all around your tongue to stimulate all your taste buds and allow the aroma to flow up the back passage to your nose. Red wine offers up to 700 compounds to taste and smell. Experienced tasters may notice smells similar to vanilla, cloves, berries, bell peppers, butter, and even soy (as a wine ages).

Notice the feeling and texture of the wine. It may be smooth on the tongue, or astringent (tannins stimulate the bitterness taste receptors as well as reduce lubrication in the mouth). It may feel full or thin (full when it has a high alcohol content, thin when low).

If you were a professional taster, you would spit out the sip to avoid imbibing too much in the course of judging, but for this experience, go ahead and swallow. Notice any changing after-taste. The wine taster takes a bite of bread or cheese between each sip to prevent habituation of the sensory cells for taste and smell. You can do this as well, which will allow you to experience the most flavor out of a glass of wine.

Shadow Dance

Light candles or another concentrated light source in a dark room. Undress, and move to your favorite music, watching your shadow on the wall copy your every move. Play with the image on the wall: turn your arms into rubber with smooth movements; make your body all pointy with elbows, knees, chin and spread fingers. Imagine you are a marionnette with a string attached to every cell; follow one string at a time, until you feel a different string pull, and follow it. Feel your balance shift and adjust no matter how you move. Close your eyes and lean, crouch, jump, or lift arms and legs, appreciating the tensile strength of your muscles and how you always know what position your body takes.

Feel the breeze you create against your skin. Swoop your face near the light, smell the burning wax or warm bulb and feel the heat against your sensitive face. When you have had your fun, turn out the light and simply sit in the dark. Experience your heartbeat, breathing, temperature, and alertness subsiding together into a relaxed you.

Engaging in Nature

Spend an afternoon hiking somewhere in nature. Even if you live in an urban area, there is probably a state or county park within a two-hour drive where you can immerse yourself in the wild. Once outdoors, engage all your senses. Here are some ideas:

- Walk barefoot and feel the different shapes and textures of the earth
- Smell wildflowers
- Crush grass or leaves for the aromatic essence
- Stand or sit still for several minutes, listening to the music of nature—leaves rustling, insects whirring, wind whistling, birds piping
- Finger the ground, plants, bark, blossoms, mushrooms—revel in texture
- Scan far vistas, including the sky
- Chew a blade of grass
- Wade in water—feel it, listen to it, see it
- Listen to the soft tamping of your feet on the path
- Feel your arms swing, thigh muscles propel, lungs expand and contract

— The Sensual Reminder —

When this book goes back onto the shelf, do not let sensuality go with it. The rush of daily life, the dulling norms, and the pressure to conform will all work against your natural sensuality, and without attention your senses may fade into utilitarian faculties. A "sensual reminder" keeps you from going too long without intentionally savoring the senses.

Choose a daily event to designate as your sensual reminder. For me, it's every time I eat. I remember to enjoy the smell, and that leads me to admiring the colors and textures, and that leads

me to noticing how my clothes feel against my skin, and then I think to listen to how my food sounds, and on and on. Those moments of sensual awareness on a regular basis keep my senses well-tuned.

The sensual reminder should be an event that you especially enjoy, one in which you probably already notice sensation. For one friend, it is the shower. His particular affinity for water reminds him to notice all his senses: the heat of the water, the sound, the feel of it hitting, the smell of shampoo, the sparkle, the slickness of skin when soapy. Yours may be when you hit the snooze in the morning, and you stretch in bed. Feel the bedclothes around you, smell the nighttime scent of yourself, savor the relaxed position of your body, and the fact that you know its position even without looking. Choose your reminder and use it every day to tune into all your senses for a moment.

Living sensually brings more peace, more interest, more wonder to your life. You have some most amazing senses just waiting to be awakened and fine tuned. You need no more money, vacation time, or education to enjoy your life more fully right now. A Saturday in your home town can be as enjoyable as a day in Tahiti if you know how to use and improve your senses.

Sensual living is following positive impulses. It's breaking a few stodgy social rules. It's running around your yard in a nightshirt, smelling an apple before you eat it, singing while you wash dishes, eating supper outside, looking at stars, going barefoot. Sensual living means loving life. Happy loving.

Bibliography

— General —

Ackerman, Diane. *A Natural History of the Senses.* New York: Random House, 1990.

Downer, John. *Supersense: Perception in the Animal World.* New York: Henry Holt and Company, 1989.

Droscher, Vitus P. *The Magic of the Senses: New Discoveries in Animal Perception.* New York: Dutton, 1969.

Rivlin, Robert and Karen Gravelle. *Deciphering the Senses: The Expanding World of Human Perception.* New York: Simon and Schuster, 1984.

— Smell —

Freedman, David H. "In the Realm of the Chemical." *Discover,* v.14 #6, June 1993.

Frye, Richard; Brian S. Schwartz, MD, and Richard L. Doty, PhD. "Dose-Related Effects of Cigarette Smoking on Olfactory Function." *Journal of the American Medical Association,* v.263 #9, March 2, 1990.

"No One's Sniffing at Smell Research Now." *Business Week,*. December 23, 1991.

"Scents of Discovery." *Town and Country,* v.143, October 1989.

Schiffman, Susan S., PhD. "Taste and Smell in Disease." *New England Journal of Medicine,* v.308 #22, June 2, 1983.

Van Toller, Steven, and George H. Dodd, editors. *Perfumery: The Psychology and Biology of Fragrance.* New York: Chapman and Hall, 1991.

— Touch —

Brooks, Charles W. *Sensory Awareness: The Rediscovery of Experiencing.* Santa Barbara: Ross-Erikson, 1974.

Gall, Sally. "Massage goes Mainstream." *American Health,* v.10, October 1991.

Gallagher, Winifred. "Touch and Balance: A Tribute to the Forgotten Senses." *American Health,* v.9 #1, Jan.-Feb. 1990.

Gunther, Bernard. *Sense Relaxation: Below Your Mind.* New York: The MacMillan Company, 1968.

Melzack, Ronald. "Phantom Limbs." *Scientific American,* v.266, April 1992.

Montagu, Ashley. *Touching: The Human Significance of the Skin.* New York and London: Columbia University Press, 1971.

Phillips, Dr. Deborah and Robert Judd. *Sexual Confidence: Discovering the Joys of Intimacy.* Boston: Houghton Mifflin, 1980.

Shreeve, James. "Touching the Phantom." *Discover,* v.14 #6, June 1993.

Szentgyorgyi, Tom. "Artificial Skin Goes on Trial." *Popular Science,* v.238, April 1991.

Weider, Betty. "Therapeutic Touch." *Shape,* v.11, March 1992.

— Taste —

Berman, Bob. "Out of the Blue." *Discover,* v.14 #6, June 1993.

Birren, Faber. *Light, Color, and the Environment.* Atglen, PA: Schiffler Publishing Ltd., 1988.

Briggs, G.A., editor and J. Moir, sub-editor. *About Your Hearing.* N.p: Rank Wharfdale Limited, 1967.

Carmer, Richard. *Our Endangered Hearing.* Emmaus, PA: Rodale Press, 1977.

Farb, Peter and Armelagos, George. *Consuming Passions: The Anthropology of Eating.* Boston: Houghton Mifflin Company, 1980.

Freedman, David H. "In the Realm of the Chemical." *Discover,* v.14 #6, June 1993.

Freese, Arthur S. *The Miracle of Vision.* New York: Harper and Row, 1977.

Godnig, Edward C., O.D. and John S. Hacunda. *Computers and Visual Stress.* Charleston, RI: Seacoast Information Services, Inc., 1990.

Grady, Denise. "The Vision Thing: Mainly in the Brain." *Discover,* v.14 #6, June 1993.

Gregg, James. *The Sportsman's Eye.* New York: Winchester Press, 1971.

Gutin, JoAnn C. "Good Vibrations." *Discover,* v.14 #6, June 1993.

Harris, Marvin. *The Sacred Cow and the Abominable Pig: Riddles of Food and Culture.* New York: Simon and Schuster, Inc., 1987.

Hearing Freese, Arthur S. *You and Your Hearing: How to Protect It, Preserve It, and Restore It.* New York: Charles Scribner's Sons, 1979.

Heuer, Kenneth. *Thunder, Singing Sands, and Other Wonders: Sound in the Atmosphere.* New York: Dodd, Mead and Company, 1981

Kamien, Roger. *Music: An Appreciation.* New York: McGraw-Hill, 1984.

Larhardt, Martin L, Ruth Skellett, Peter Wang, and Alex M. Clarke. "Human Ultrasonic Speech Perception." *Science,* v.253, July 5, 1991.

Lewis, Ricki PhD. "When Taste and Smell Go Awry." *FDA Consumer,* v.25 #9, November 1991.

Logue, A.W. *The Psychology and Biology of Eating and Drinking.* New York: W.H. Freeman and Company, 1986.

Mueller, Conrad G. and Mae Rudolph and the editors of *Life. Light and Vision.* New York: Time Incorporated, 1966.

Neal, Helen. *Low Vision: What You Can Do To Preserve-and Even Enhance- Your Usable Eyesight.* New York: Simon and Schuster, 1987.

The Monell Connection Newsletter, Spring 1992.

"The Musical Brain." *US News and World Report,* v.108 #23, June 11, 1990.

Vision Anshel, Jeffrey, M.D. *Healthy Eyes, Better Vision: Everyday Eye Care for the Whole Family.* Los Angeles: The Body Press, 1990.

— ESP —

Frazier, Kendrick, editor. *The Hundredth Monkey and Other Paradigms of the Paranormal.* Buffalo, NY: Prometheus Books, 1991.

Gottlieb, Annie. "How To Make Decisions You Won't Forget." *McCalls,* June 1992.

Holzer, Hans. *The Truth About ESP.* Garden City, NY: Doubleday and Co., Inc., 1974.

Koestler, Arthur. *The Roots of Coincidence.* New York: Random House, 1972.

Kreskin. *Secrets of the Amazing Kreskin.* Buffalo, New York: Prometheus Books, 1991.

Logan, Daniel. *Do You Have ESP.* Garden City, New York: Doubleday and Co., Inc., 1970.

Nash, Carroll B., PhD. *Parapsychology: The Science of Psiology.* Gettysburg, PA: Thomas Publications, 1986.

Watson, Lyall. *Beyond Supernature: A New Natural History of the Supernatural.* New York: Bantam Books, 1988.

On the following pages you will find listed, with their current prices, some of the books now available on related subjects. Your book dealer stocks most of these and will stock new titles in the Llewellyn series as they become available. We urge your patronage.

TO GET A FREE CATALOG

You are invited to write for our bi-monthly news magazine/catalog, *Llewellyn's New Worlds of Mind and Spirit*. A sample copy is free, and it will continue coming to you at no cost as long as you are an active mail customer. Or you may subscribe for just $10 in the United States and Canada ($20 overseas, first class mail). Many bookstores also have *New Worlds* available to their customers. Ask for it.

In *New Worlds* you will find news and features about new books, tapes and services; announcements of meetings and seminars; helpful articles; author interviews and much more. Write to:

Llewellyn's New Worlds of Mind and Spirit
P.O. Box 64383-K160, St. Paul, MN 55164-0383, U.S.A.

TO ORDER BOOKS AND TAPES

If your book store does not carry the titles described on the following pages, you may order them directly from Llewellyn by sending the full price in U.S. funds, plus postage and handling (see below).

Credit card orders: VISA, MasterCard, American Express are accepted. Call us toll-free within the United States and Canada at 1-800-THE-MOON.

Special Group Discount: Because there is a great deal of interest in group discussion and study of the subject matter of this book, we offer a 20% quantity discount to group leaders or agents. Our Special Quantity Price for a minimum order of five copies of *Sensuous Living* is $51.80 cash-with-order. Include postage and handling charges noted below.

Postage and Handling: Include $4 postage and handling for orders $15 and under; $5 for orders *over* $15. There are no postage and handling charges for orders over $100. Postage and handling rates are subject to change. We ship UPS whenever possible within the continental United States; delivery is guaranteed. Please provide your street address as UPS does not deliver to P.O. boxes. Orders shipped to Alaska, Hawaii, Canada, Mexico and Puerto Rico will be sent via first class mail. Allow 4-6 weeks for delivery. **International orders:** Airmail – add retail price of each book and $5 for each non-book item (audiotapes, etc.); Surface mail – add $1 per item.

Minnesota residents add 7% sales tax.

Mail orders to:
Llewellyn Worldwide, P.O. Box 64383-K160, St. Paul, MN 55164-0383, U.S.A.
For customer service, call (612) 291-1970.

HOLISTIC AROMATHERAPY
Balance the Body and Soul with Essential Oils
by Ann Berwick

For thousands of years, aromatherapy—the therapeutic use of the essential oils of aromatic plants—has been used for the benefit of mankind. These oils are highly concentrated forms of herbal energy that represent the soul, or life force, of the plant. When the aromatic vapor is inhaled, it can influence areas of the brain inaccessible to conscious control such as emotions and hormonal responses. Application of the oils in massage can enhance the benefits of body work on the muscular, lymphatic and nervous systems. By cutaneous application of the oils, we can influence more deeply the main body systems.

This is the first complete guide to holistic aromatherapy—what it is, how and why it works. Written from the perspective of a practicing aromatherapist, *Holistic Aromatherapy* provides insights into the magic of creating body balance through the use of individually blended oils, and it offers professional secrets of working with these potent substances on the physical, mental, emotional and spiritual levels.

0-87542-033-8, 240 pgs., 6 x 9, illus., softcover   **$12.95**

THE SECRET OF LETTING GO
by Guy Finley
Whether you need to let go of a painful
heartache, a destructive habit, a frightening
worry or a nagging discontent, *The Secret of
Letting Go* shows you how to call upon your
own hidden powers and how they can take
you through and beyond any challenge or
problem. This book reveals the secret source
of a brand-new kind of inner strength.

In the light of your new and higher self-
understanding, emotional difficulties such as loneliness, fear, anxiety and frustration fade into nothingness as you happily discover
they never really existed in the first place.

With a foreword by Desi Arnaz Jr., and introduction by Dr. Jesse
Freeland, *The Secret of Letting Go* is a pleasing balance of questions
and answers, illustrative examples, truth tales, and stimulating dia-
logues that allow the reader to share in the exciting discoveries that
lead up to lasting self-liberation.

This is a book for the discriminating, intelligent, and sensitive
reader who is looking for *real* answers.
0-87542-223-3, 240 pgs., 5¼ x 8, softcover   **$9.95**

All prices subject to change without notice

THE SECRET WAY OF WONDER
Insights from the Silence
by Guy Finley
Introduction by Desi Arnaz, Jr.
Discover an inner world of wisdom and make miracles happen! Here is a simple yet deeply effective system of illuminating and eliminating the problems of inner mental and emotional life.

The Secret Way of Wonder is an interactive spiritual workbook, offering guided practice for self-study. It is about Awakening the Power of Wonder in yourself. A series of 60 "Wonders" (meditations on a variety of subjects: "The Wonder of Change," "The Wonder of Attachments," etc.) will stir you in an indescribable manner. This is a bold and bright new kind of book that gently leads us on a journey of Spiritual Alchemy where the journey itself is the destination ... and the destination is our need to be spiritually whole men and women.

Most of all, you will find out through self investigation that we live in a friendly, intelligent and living universe that we can reach into and that can reach us.
0-87542-221-7, 192 pgs., 5¼ x 8, softcover   **$9.95**

All prices subject to change without notice

FREEDOM FROM THE TIES THAT BIND
The Secret of Self Liberation
by Guy Finley

Imagine how your life would flow *without* the weight of those weary inner voices constantly convincing you that "you can't," or complaining that someone else should be blamed for the way *you* feel. The weight of the world on your shoulders would be replaced by a bright, new sense of freedom. Fresh, new energies would flow. *You could choose to live the way YOU want.* In *Freedom from the Ties that Bind*, Guy Finley reveals hundreds of Celestial, but down-to-earth, secrets of Self-Liberation that show you exactly how to be fully independent, and *free of any condition not to your liking*. Even the most difficult people won't be able to turn your head or test your temper. Enjoy solid, meaningful relationships founded *in conscious choice*—not *through self-defeating compromise.* Learn the secrets of unlocking the door to your own Free Mind. Be empowered to break free of any self-punishing pattern, and make the discovery that who you really are is already everything you've ever wanted to be.

0-87542-217-9, 240 pgs., 6 x 9, softcover $10.00

All prices subject to change without notice